Finally, a cc
A COURSE IN MIRA
Jesus tried to g⌐

MW01531139

BIBLICAL QUOTES FROM
A COURSE IN
MIRACLES
REINTERPRETED

GENE SKAGGS, JR.

Author of A Beginner's Glossary to A COURSE IN MIRACLES,
The Relationship Game, and
101 Questions and Answers on the Course

Copyright © 2008 by Gene Skaggs, Jr.

All rights reserved. No part of this book may be reproduced, stored in a retrieval system, or transmitted in any form or by any means—electronic, mechanical, photocopying, recording, or any other—except for brief quotations in printed reviews, without prior written permission of the publisher.

Published by One Miracle

First edition 2007

ISBN 978-0-9800049-0-8

Printed in the United States of America

CONTENTS

ACKNOWLEDGMENTS

I would like to acknowledge my great indebtedness to First Church Unity of Nashville, Tennessee, for helping me find a vision of God in the Bible that I could accept and ultimately cherish.

Before Unity I never felt a connection to the Bible because of all the hell-fire information I had heard from organized religion. One of the main reasons I was attracted to Unity was the way they depicted a loving God with metaphysical interpretations of the Bible that were highly relevant to me and our 21st Century world. Charles Fillmore, one of the founders of Unity Church said, "The Bible is a very wonderful book; as man develops in spiritual understanding it reveals itself to him, and he sees why it has been reverenced and called holy by the people."

Soon after attending Unity I was introduced to A COURSE IN MIRACLES where I discovered more ideas about the Bible that were harmonious with Unity's approach. I began to discover that the healing and empowering messages in both Unity and A COURSE IN MIRACLES were also in the Bible and that the hell-fire information that had distanced me was simply mistaken.

I believe there are numerous people who really don't resonate with the hell-fire view but still have a great longing for the Bible and Jesus. What I have done in this book on A COURSE IN MIRACLES, is to take biblical references and show how the Course gives them an entirely different meaning. You will see that the messages are more gentle and loving than the way they have been presented in traditional Biblical interpretation.

First Church Unity helped me find A COURSE IN MIRACLES and both of them helped me find God in the Bible.

I would also like to thank Rev. Cherie Larkin at First Church Unity for allowing a variety of alternative classes, including A COURSE IN MIRACLES. For 20 years this church has been the Nashville homesite of the class on A COURSE IN MIRACLES which I facilitate every Tuesday night and Sunday morning.

And, finally, I would like to thank Janice Mickle for the first editing, and my mother, Charo Hacker for reading and commenting on this manuscript. Her constant loving support of my association with Unity Church and my work with A COURSE IN MIRACLES is deeply cherished.

What I have done in this, my fourth book on A COURSE IN MIRACLES, is to take biblical references and show how the Course gives them an entirely different meaning. As you will see, a more gentle and loving interpretation than the way it has been presented to the masses.

This book is in NO way meant to compare the Course with other thought systems, nor is it meant to make the Course right and the Bible wrong. As the Course states, "There is a course for every teacher of God. The form of the course varies greatly. So do the particular teaching aids involved. This is a manual for a special curriculum, intended for teachers of a special form of the universal course. There are many thousands of other forms, all with the same outcome."

I will use only direct quotes from the Bible, or where the Course says the Bible states a specific idea, or when there is some specific reference to the Bible. The only exception to the above guidelines are the words which are now common Christian words that didn't exist during the time Jesus walked the planet. Two examples would be Christmas and Easter. The reason I have chosen to use only these four criteria for this book is to avoid personal interpretation as to where the statements are made as references to the Bible. Hopefully, this will avoid controversy in this area. Some references will be referred to more than once. The reason for this is that they are referred to in different places in the Course with added insight.

It is my hope that this book will NOT inspire anyone to take a stand on one side or the other. There is only one Bible; however, look at all the different religions that base their doctrines on the teaching of this book. Many have different interpretations, and all use the same book.

Just about every word that we use in our English language has at least two meanings. That doesn't make one definition right and the other wrong. A nice example of that would be the word "mouse". If you are on the computer that word has one meaning, and our little creature crawling around on the floor has quite a different meaning.

After each quote from the Bible, I will give you exactly what A COURSE IN MIRACLES says about it. After that I will put my name, "Gene," and elaborate on it in more detail to help expand on the Course's interpretation.

The purpose of this book is to show that there is another more loving way of looking at the message our elder brother was trying to get across to us over two thousand years ago.

As Jesus says in the Course "I came to fulfill the law by reinterpreting it."

CHAPTER 1

Text, page 7: "No man cometh unto the Father but by me."

A COURSE IN MIRACLES interpretation: "You are a perfect creation, and should experience awe only in the presence of the Creator of perfection. The miracle is therefore a sign of love among equals. Equals should not be in awe of one another because awe implies inequality. It is therefore an inappropriate reaction to me. An elder brother is entitled to respect for his greater experience, and obedience for his greater wisdom. He is also entitled to love because he is a brother, and to devotion if he is devoted. It is only my devotion that entitles me to yours. There is nothing about me that you cannot attain. I have nothing that does not come from God. The difference between us now is that I have nothing else. This leaves me in a state which is only potential in you.

This does not mean that I/Jesus am in any way separate or different from you except in time. The statement is more meaningful in terms of a vertical rather than a horizontal axis. You stand below me and I stand below God. In the process of "rising up," I am higher because without me the distance between God and man would be too great for you to encompass."

Gene: Jesus tells us in the above quote that he is our equal, although he does make a distinction. He tells us that he has no ego, a state that is only potential in us. The difference between Jesus and us is that he recognizes his total allegiance to God; we don't. Because of this, he can bring us up to his level where we become fully aware of our oneness with our Creator. He is referred to as an elder brother. An elder brother can show you things that he can do and guides you in attaining those same qualities.

CHAPTER 2

Text, page 8: "I and my Father are one."

A COURSE IN MIRACLES interpretation: "There are two parts to the statement in recognition that the Father is greater."

Gene: Jesus is, in fact, one with God. We are one with Jesus; and, therefore, we are one with God. This statement is not meant to be read as Jesus having an exclusive right to the oneness with our Creator. If we are Jesus's equal then, as he tells us, we are one with our Creator. Again, the only difference is he recognizes his total dependence to God; while we don't.

CHAPTER 3

Text, page 9: "Heaven and earth shall pass away."

A COURSE IN MIRACLES interpretation: "Means that they will not continue to exist as separate states."

Gene: Right now, we feel there are two voices fighting to get through to us. It is up to us to choose to only listen to the loving Voice of God. The ultimate goal is to listen to this Voice exclusively. This will be the total removal of our ego thoughts. With our ego thoughts removed, separate thoughts become impossible. We will now be in the state referred to in the Course as the "real world". This simply means we have a body, but our thoughts are totally one with our Creator, as Jesus was, and is.

CHAPTER 4

Text, page 9: "Resurrection and the life."

A COURSE IN MIRACLES interpretation: "My word, which is the resurrection and the life, shall not pass away because life is eternal. You are the work of God, and His work is wholly lovable and wholly loving. This is how a man must think of himself in his heart, because this is what he is."

Gene: When Jesus says "My word" he is referring to those divine Thoughts he received from God. We, too, are just as capable of hearing the Voice of God because He is constantly speaking to us. The Course states that if we can't hear the Voice for God, it is we who are not listening.

It is like not having the radio on, and then complaining you can't hear the song they are currently playing. Put down your grievances, your judgments, and then you can hear the mighty Voice for God. When we hear the Voice for God, we feel alive; and when we listen to our ego, we feel something less than whole.

CHAPTER 5

Text, page 9: "Lead us not into temptation."

A COURSE IN MIRACLES interpretation: "Recognize your errors and choose to abandon them by following my guidance."

Gene: God will never lead us into any situation that would cause us pain. God is Love, and the only thing that can emanate from Love is Love. It is insane to think that Love would punish you because you were bad, punish you to teach you a lesson, or cause you pain to guide you to do a certain thing. We, our ego thoughts, have this insane belief that by punishing ourselves we can atone for the "sins" we feel we have committed. Notice the word the Course used in the explanation. The word used is "errors," not sins. Errors, as the Course states, call for correction; sin, if real, would call for punishment.

CHAPTER 6

Text, page 10: "Golden Rule"

A COURSE IN MIRACLES interpretation: "You respond to what you perceive, and as you perceive so shall you behave. The Golden Rule asks you to do unto others as you would have them do unto you. This means that the perception of both must be accurate. You cannot behave appropriately unless you perceive correctly. Since you and your neighbor are equal members of one family, as you perceive both so you will do to both. You should look out from the perception of your own holiness to the holiness of others."

Gene: The Golden Rule tells us that we have to perceive properly so that our response will always be love. There are only two interpretations one can make about another. One is your brothers or sisters are expressing love; and the other response would be a cry for help. Either way, the response to the interpretation is love.

With love now in my mind I recognize my brothers and sisters are of the same family and I am one with them, my view of them is my view of myself. My fears are a cry for help; and, therefore, their fears mirror my cry for help. If you want to know where you are on your ladder back to God, just look at your brothers and sisters and ask yourself, "What is my opinion of them?" That opinion of them will be your opinion of yourself.

CHAPTER 7

Text, page 11: "There is no death."

A COURSE IN MIRACLES interpretation: "The emptiness engendered by fear must be replaced by forgiveness. This is what the Bible means by "There is no death," and why I could demonstrate that death does not exist. I came to fulfill the law by reinterpreting it. The law itself, if properly understood, offers only protection. It is those who have not yet changed their minds who brought the "hell-fire" concept into it. Your witnessing demonstrates your belief, and thus strengthens it. Those who witness for me are expressing, through their miracles, that they have abandoned the belief in deprivation in favor of the abundance they have learned belongs to them."

Gene: When the Course refers to death, very seldom are they referring to the definition that we all are familiar with. The vast majority of times when the Course uses the word "death" they are referring to the fact that any ego thought we have is a death thought. So when Jesus says he had overcome death, what he is referring to is that he no longer has any ego thoughts. His thought system is in total alignment with our Creator. From a biblical perspective, he showed us that even though the body may be laid aside, communication remains unbroken.

CHAPTER 8

Text, page 12: "Except ye become as little children."

A COURSE IN MIRACLES interpretation: "Means that unless you fully recognize your complete dependence on God, you cannot know the real power of the Son in his true relationships with the Father."

Gene: Jesus could only listen to the One Voice; and, therefore, he was like a little child. He knew where his Source came from, and is trying to implore us to be like children who listen only to the Voice of God. We have to come to the realization that God is the Source of our supply in all areas of our life. Others are just a vortex for God's unlimited bounty.

CHAPTER 9

Text, page 13: "God is not mocked."

A COURSE IN MIRACLES interpretation: "Is not a warning but a reassurance. God would be mocked if any of His creations lacked holiness. The creation is whole, and the mark of wholeness is holiness. Miracles are affirmations of the Sonship, which is a state of completion and abundance."

Gene: Isn't that a more loving way to look at what was said in the Bible? Instead of looking at that passage as one that instills the fear of God, it simply states that all His children are to be loving to one another, just like Him. In fact, all we are is Love.

CHAPTER 10

Text, page 13: "Shallow roots"

A COURSE IN MIRACLES interpretation: "The miracle is a sign that the mind has chosen to be led by me in Christ's service. The abundance of Christ is the natural result of choosing to follow Him. All shallow roots must be uprooted, because they are not deep enough to sustain you. The illusion that shallow roots can be deepened, and thus made to hold, is one of the distortions on which the reverse of the Golden Rules rests. As these false underpinnings are given up, the equilibrium is temporarily experienced as unstable. However, nothing is less stable than an upside-down orientation. Nor can anything that holds it upside down be conducive to increased stability."

Gene: Shallow roots are referring to your ego thought system, and those thoughts will not sustain you.

CHAPTER 11

Text, page 13: "Fall"

A COURSE IN MIRACLES interpretation: "You who want peace can find it only by complete forgiveness. No learning is acquired by anyone unless he wants to learn it and believes in some way that he needs it. While lack does not exist in the creation of God, it is very apparent in what you have made. It is, in fact, the essential difference between them. Lack implies that you would be better off in a state somehow different from the one you are in. Until the "separation," which is the meaning of the "fall," nothing was lacking. There were no needs at all. Needs arise only when you deprive yourself. You act according to the particular order of needs you establish. This, in turn, depends on your perception of what you are."

Gene: The "Fall" is made in references to separation. The separation can be the cosmic separation from God, or the separation from our brothers and sisters, or the separation from our good. All separation from our good comes from the belief that we have separated from God, and this "sin" makes us feel bad. If we feel bad, we are not in alignment with God; and therefore, we deprive ourselves of our good. What heals the separation/fall is forgiveness.

CHAPTER 12

Text, page 17: "Detour into fear."

A COURSE IN MIRACLES interpretation: "These related distortions represent a picture of what actually occurred in the separation, or the "detour into fear." None of this existed before the separation, nor does it actually exist now. Everything God created is like Him. Extension, as undertaken by God, is similar to the inner radiance that the children of the Father inherit from Him. Its real source is internal. This is as true of the Son as of the Father. In this sense the creation includes both the creation of the Son by God, and the Son's creations when his mind is healed. This requires God's endowment of the Son with free will, because all loving creation is freely given in one continuous line, in which all aspects are of the same order."

Gene: Detour into fear simply means the instant we listen to our ego thoughts we have made a detour from the God part of us.

CHAPTER 13

Text, page 17: "Garden of Eden"

A COURSE IN MIRACLES interpretation: "The Garden of Eden, or the pre-separation condition, was a state of mind in which nothing was needed."

Gene: The Garden of Eden refers to our total oneness with God. In this state we have no needs, no worries or lacks. We are literally one with everything.

CHAPTER 14

Text, page 17: "Lies of the serpent."

A COURSE IN MIRACLES interpretation: "When Adam listened to the "lies of the serpent," all he heard was untruth. You do not have to continue to believe what is not true unless you choose to do so."

Gene: The lies of the serpent refers to our ego thoughts.

CHAPTER 15

Text, page 18: "Deep sleep fell upon Adam."

A COURSE IN MIRACLES interpretation: "What is seen in dreams seems to be very real. Yet the Bible says that a deep sleep fell upon Adam, and nowhere is there reference to his waking up. The world has not yet experienced any comprehensive reawakening or rebirth. Such a rebirth is impossible as long as you continue to project or miscreate. It still remains within you, however, to extend as God extended His spirit to you. In reality this is your only choice, because your free will was given you for your joy in creating the perfect."

Gene: The word "dream" is another one of the words used in the Course that is given a totally different meaning than we are used to using. Until we have removed our ego thought system completely, the Course says each thought we have is a dream. When we listen to the ego, we are having nightmare dreams, and when we are listening to the Holy Spirit, we are having a happy dream. But they are still dreams, because even in the happy dreams, we have the choice to have a dream/thought that will pull us from the happy dream. Only in our total alignment with our Creator are we truly awake.

CHAPTER 16

Text, page 20: "The meek shall inherit the earth."

A COURSE IN MIRACLES interpretation: "The Atonement is the total commitment. You may still think this is associated with loss, a mistake all the separated Sons of God make in one way or another. It is hard to believe a defense that cannot attack is the best defense. This is what is meant by "the meek shall inherit the earth." They will literally take it over because of their strength."

Gene: The meek are the ones who have realized that strength comes from their defenselessness. By listening to the Voice for God you are energized and feel the strength in every cell of your being. The more that we come to this realization, the more we can help those who believe strength comes from listening to their ego. Then we will have complete dominion over the earth instead of feeling that the earth is the determiner of how I feel. This defenselessness is similar to Unity's law of non-resistance.

CHAPTER 17

Text, page 28: "Father forgive them for they know not what they do."

A COURSE IN MIRACLES interpretation: "Miracle-minded forgiveness is only correction. It has no element of judgment at all. The statement "Father forgive them for they know not what they do" in no way evaluates what they do. It is an appeal to God to heal their minds. There is no reference to the outcome of the error. That does not matter."

Gene: This one will be hard if you are trying to interpret it with your old definition of forgiveness. Forgiveness is a change of mind from listening to our ego to listening to the Holy Spirit. Jesus is telling us to listen to the Voice for God, and only then will we be able to experience the true forgiveness God has for all of us.

True forgiveness corrects the problem where it truly takes place—the mind. Once this has happened, one will be guided what to do at the form level. This guidance will always be beneficial for both the giver of forgiveness, as well as the receiver.

CHAPTER 18

Text, page 28: "Be of one mind."

A COURSE IN MIRACLES interpretation: "The injunction "Be of one mind" is the statement for revelation-readiness."

Gene: To be of one mind means to listen to the dualistic part of our mind that is connected to God.

CHAPTER 19

Text, page 28: "Do this in remembrance of me."

A COURSE IN MIRACLES interpretation: "My request "Do this in remembrance of me" is the appeal for cooperation from miracle workers. This statement involves an awareness of time, since to remember is to recall the past in the present. Time is under my direction, but timelessness belongs to God. In time we exist for and with each other. In timelessness we coexist with God."

Gene: What Jesus wants from us is to listen to the Voice that he listens to, and then you truly will remember him.

CHAPTER 20

**Text, page 33: "For God so loved the world
that He gave His only begotten Son,
that whosoever believeth in him
should not perish but have everlasting life."**

A COURSE IN MIRACLES interpretation: "This statement needs only one slight correction to be meaningful in this context; "He gave it to His only begotten Son."

Gene: What a major difference from the way this statement has been interpreted. What the Course means simply is: that God so Loved what He created, that He gave His Love to each and every one of us. God's only begotten Son is not just Jesus, but all of us. We all make up the Son, or as it is referred to at times, as the Sonship.

CHAPTER 21

Text, page 34: "Last Judgment"

A COURSE IN MIRACLES interpretation: "The Last Judgment is one of the most threatening ideas in your thinking. This is because you do not understand it. Judgment is not an attribute of God. It was brought into being only after the separation, when it became one of the many learning devices to be built into the overall plan. Just as the separation occurred over millions of years, the Last Judgment will extend over a similarly long period, and perhaps an even longer one. Its length can, however, be greatly shortened by miracles, the device for shortening but not abolishing time. If a sufficient number become truly miracle-minded, this shortening process can be virtually immeasurable. It is essential, however, that you free yourself from fear quickly, because you must emerge from the conflict if you are to bring peace to other minds.

The Last Judgment is generally thought of as a procedure undertaken by God. Actually it will be undertaken by my brothers with my help. It is a final healing rather than a meting out of punishment, however much you may think that punishment is deserved. Punishment is a concept totally opposed to right-mindedness. The Last Judgment might be called a process of right evaluation. It simply means that everyone will finally come to understand what is worthy and what is not. After this, the ability to choose can be directed rationally. Until this distinction is made, however, the vacillations between free and imprisoned will cannot but continue. The term "Last Judgment" is frightening not only because it has been projected onto God, but also because of the association of "last" with death. This is an outstanding example of upside-down perception. If the meaning of the Last Judgment is objectively examined, it is quite apparent that it is really the doorway to life. No one who lives in fear is really alive."

Gene: The Last Judgment is frightening because of the way it has been portrayed for two main reasons. First, "last" being associated with death; and also, that God would finally judge those that were good and those that were bad and reward or punish accordingly. It is simply the time when we finally come to understand completely who we are as a child of God. When we arrive at that internal knowing, there is never an instant in which we will listen to the ego ever again.

CHAPTER 22

Text, page 34: "Apocalypse"

A COURSE IN MIRACLES interpretation: "The first step toward freedom involves a sorting out of the false from the true. This is a process of separation in the constructive sense, and reflects the true meaning of the Apocalypse. Everyone will ultimately look upon his own creations and choose to preserve only what is good, just as God Himself looked upon what He had created and knew that it was good. At this point, the mind can begin to look with love on its own creations because of their worthiness. At the same time the mind will inevitably disown its miscreations which, without belief, will no longer exist."

Gene: This is the process we go through in looking at both our loving thoughts and those that are not so loving. When we finally realize that only the thoughts for God represent who we are, then we will no longer desire other thoughts.

Text, page 36: "Crucifixion" and "Resurrection"

A COURSE IN MIRACLES interpretation: "A further point must be perfectly clear before any residual fear still associated with miracles can disappear. The crucifixion did not establish the Atonement; the resurrection did. Many sincere Christians have misunderstood this. No one who is free of the belief in scarcity could possibly make this mistake. If the crucifixion is seen from an upside-down point of view, it does appear as if God permitted and even encouraged one of His Sons to suffer because he was good. This particularly unfortunate interpretation, which arose out of projection, has led many people to be bitterly afraid of God. Such anti-religious concepts enter into many religions. Yet the real Christian should pause and ask, "How could this be?" Is it likely that God Himself would be capable of the kind of thinking which His Own words have clearly stated is unworthy of His Son?

Persecution frequently results in an attempt to "justify" the terrible misperception that God Himself persecuted His Own Son on behalf of salvation. The very words are meaningless. It has been particularly difficult to overcome this because many have been unwilling to give it up in view of its prominent value as a defense. In milder forms a parent says "This hurts me more than it hurts you," and feels exonerated in beating a child. Can you believe your Father really thinks this way? It is so essential that all such thinking be dispelled that we must be sure that nothing of this kind remains in your mind. I WAS NOT "PUNISHED" (caps by

Gene) because you were bad. The wholly benign lesson the Atonement teaches is lost if it is tainted with this kind of distortion in any form."

Gene: Crucifixion means any ego thought, and resurrection means any thought we have with God.

CHAPTER 24

Text, page 36: "Vengeance is mine, sayeth the Lord."

A COURSE IN MIRACLES interpretation: "This is a misperception by which one assigns his own "evil" past to God. The "evil" past has nothing to do with God. He did not create it and He does not maintain it. God does not believe in retribution. Is it likely that He would hold them against me? Be very sure that you recognize how utterly impossible this assumption is, and how entirely it arises from projection."

Gene: God is only Love; therefore, vengeance cannot be of God. What God wants from us is our vengeance, so She can remove it. That's what God means, give God all your thoughts that do not mirror God's.

CHAPTER 25

Text, page 37: "God rejected Adam and forced him out of the Garden of Eden."

A COURSE IN MIRACLES interpretation: "God does not hold your "evil" deeds against you. Is it likely that He would hold them against me? Be very sure that you recognize how utterly impossible this assumption is, and how entirely it arises from projection. This kind of error is responsible for a host of related errors, including the belief that God rejected Adam and forced him out of the Garden of Eden. It is also why you may believe from time to time that I am misdirecting you."

Gene: Basically, the Course is saying God did not say what was supposedly quoted by Her. This could only come about by man making God in their image. When mankind uses the limited part of their minds, the ego, they will always reject others and force them out of their lives. So, very naturally, man projected the forced exile of Adam onto God so man could feel good about rejecting others.

CHAPTER 26

Text, page 37: "The lamb of God who taketh away the sins of the world."

A COURSE IN MIRACLES interpretation: "I have been correctly referred to as "the lamb of God who taketh away the sins of the world," but those who represent the lamb as blood-stained do not understand the meaning of the symbol. Correctly understood, it is a very simple symbol that speaks of my innocence. The lion and the lamb lying down together symbolize that strength and innocence are not in conflict, but naturally live in peace.

Innocence is incapable of sacrificing anything, because the innocent mind has everything and strives only to protect its wholeness. It cannot project. It can only honor other minds, because honor is the natural greeting of the truly loved to others who are like them. The lamb "taketh away the sins of the world" in the sense that the state of innocence, or grace, is one in which the meaning of the Atonement is perfectly apparent."

Gene: Jesus can be looked at as a bridge from where we think things happen in the external world to his love in our mind, where everything really takes place. Jesus is like a middle man. We give him our sins - technically speaking the word should be "mistakes" - because we really cannot commit sins; and Jesus removes those erroneous thoughts and replaces them with loving thoughts.

CHAPTER 27

Text, page 37: "Lion and the lamb"

A COURSE IN MIRACLES interpretation: "The lion and the lamb lying down together symbolize that strength and innocence are not in conflict, but naturally live in peace. "Blessed are the pure in heart for they shall see God" is another way of saying the same thing. A pure mind knows the truth and this is its strength. It does not confuse destruction with innocence because it associates innocence with strength, not with weakness."

Gene: We usually don't associate spiritual thoughts and acts as strength. Most people look at them as something God wants us to do, and at times feelings of obligation might be felt. We usually look at strength as someone overcoming great external odds. True strength comes from listening and following the Loving Voice of God. That type of strength entails no strain on our part. The lamb represents peace, and listening to the Voice for God will give us peace. Now we can experience strength and peace because they are actually one and the same.

CHAPTER 28

**Text, page 37: "Blessed are the pure in heart
for they shall see God."**

A COURSE IN MIRACLES interpretation: "A pure mind
knows the truth about this is its strength. It does not confuse
destruction with innocence because it associates innocence
with strength, not with weakness."

Gene: A pure mind is a quiet mind, a mind that listens and
knows its oneness with its Creator.

CHAPTER 29

Text, page 39: "Holy Trinity"

A COURSE IN MIRACLES interpretation: "Nothing can prevail against a Son of God who commends his spirit into the Hands of his Father. By doing this the mind awakens from its sleep and remembers its Creator. All sense of separation disappears. The Son of God is part of the Holy Trinity, but the Trinity Itself is one. There are no confusions within Its Levels, because They are of one Mind and one Will. This single purpose creates perfect integration and establishes the peace of God."

Gene: There are three parts to the Holy Trinity, but they are not separate parts. Each part is connected to the other and each part sees no separation from the other. This will probably be hard to grasp because we are trying to understand Oneness using our split mind. God, Holy Spirit, and Jesus are one in that they all have the same purpose. This purpose is to help you recognize who you are as a loving child of God. With this realization we feel our oneness with all our brothers and sisters as well as every living thing on this planet. One might want to view this as there are different cells in our body that seem to be separate from one another, but they are all connected in one way or another.

CHAPTER 30

Text, page 39: "When he shall appear or be perceived we shall be like him, for we shall see him as he is."

A COURSE IN MIRACLES interpretation: "The Son of God is part of the Holy Trinity, but the Trinity Itself is one. This single purpose creates perfect integration and establishes the peace of God. Yet this vision can be perceived only by the truly innocent. Because their hearts are pure, the innocent defend true perception instead of defending themselves against it. Understanding the lesson of the Atonement they are without the wish to attack, and therefore they see truly. This is what the Bible means when it says, "When he shall appear (or be perceived) we shall be like him, for we shall see him as he is."

Gene: When we are purely innocent, which means we no longer have an ego, then we will see only love expressing itself in everyone. The reason for this is love will be the only thought that will be in our mind. Therefore, we will mirror our elder brother, Jesus, and our perception will be like his.

CHAPTER 31

Text, page 40: "Know yourself"

A COURSE IN MIRACLES interpretation: "The Bible tells you to know yourself, or to be certain. Certainty is always of God. When you love someone you have perceived him as he is, and this makes it possible for you to know him. Until you first perceive him as he is you cannot know him."

Gene: To know yourself, to know God, to know your brothers and sisters means to know the God part of everyone and everything. When one is in touch with this, then one will see only that in others.

CHAPTER 32

Text, page 41: "Alpha and Omega"

A COURSE IN MIRACLES interpretation: "Right perception is necessary before God can communicate directly to His altars, which He established in His Sons. There He can communicate His certainty, and His knowledge will bring peace without question. God is not a stranger to His Sons, and His Sons are not strangers to each other. Knowledge preceded both perception and time, and will ultimately replace them. That is the real meaning of "Alpha and Omega, the beginning and the end," and "Before Abraham was I am."

Gene: When we only have thoughts that mirror those of God, we will be like Her. In that state, we are one because there is no separation.

CHAPTER 33

Text, page 41: "Before Abraham was I am."

A COURSE IN MIRACLES interpretation: "Right perception is necessary before God can communicate directly to His altars, which He established in His Sons. There He can communicate His certainty, and His knowledge will bring peace without question. God is not a stranger to His Sons, and His Sons are not strangers to each other. Knowledge preceded both perception and time, and will ultimately replace them. Knowledge is the real meaning of "Alpha and Omega, the beginning and the end," and "Before Abraham was I am."

Gene: Not until we are seeing things through the eyes of God can we communicate with God. God is not a stranger to us, nor are we a stranger to our brothers and sisters. Before we can recognize our oneness, we have to be listening exclusively to the Voice for God.

CHAPTER 34

Text, page 41: "Fear God and keep His commandments."

A COURSE IN MIRACLES interpretation: "Fear God and keep His commandments" becomes Know God and accept His certainty."

Gene: A lovely way to look at a passage in the Bible differently. It says that once we know that God is Love and only wants joy and peace for us, why would we not listen to His Word and keep His commandments.

CHAPTER 35

Text, page 43: "Many are called but few are chosen."

A COURSE IN MIRACLES interpretation: "God and His creations remain in surety, and therefore know that no miscreation exists. Truth cannot deal with errors that you want. I was a man who remembered spirit and its knowledge. As a man I did not attempt to counteract error with knowledge, but to correct error from the bottom up. I demonstrated both the powerlessness of the body and the power of the mind. By uniting my will with that of my Creator, I naturally remembered spirit and its real purpose. I cannot unite your will with God's for you, but I can erase all misperceptions from your mind if you will bring it under my guidance. Only your misperceptions stand in your way. Without them your choice is certain. Sane perception induces sane choosing. I cannot chose for you, but I can help you make your own right choice. "Many are called but few are chosen" should be, "All are called but few choose to listen."

Gene: God's call is universal, its extension is endless. This love is constant, it never changes because of circumstances. When one brother or sister accepts this Call this Love extends to all the Sonship. Individual acceptance is possible, as in the case of Jesus and numerous others. Those that have chosen to hear the call are the "chosen ones." When that occurs they recognize who they are as a child of God.

CHAPTER 36

Text, page 44: "Chosen ones"

A COURSE IN MIRACLES interpretation: "The "chosen ones" are merely those who choose right sooner."

Gene: The Course tells us that we are all the "chosen ones." The only difference between the "chosen ones" and the others is the "chosen ones" recognize their complete oneness with God.

CHAPTER 37

Text, page 45: "God created man in his own image and likeness."

A COURSE IN MIRACLES interpretation: "Image can be understood as "thoughts," and "likeness" as "of a like quality." God did create spirit in His Own Thought and of a quality like to His Own."

Gene: We are the thought of God and of like quality. Because of this, our creative power of connection to Source can never diminish.

Text, page 46: "Judge not that ye be not judged."

A COURSE IN MIRACLE interpretation: "We have already discussed the Last Judgment but in insufficient detail. After the Last Judgment there will be no more. Judgment is symbolic because beyond perception there is no judgment. When the Bible says "Judge not that ye be not judged," it means that if you judge the reality of others you will be unable to avoid judging your own.

The choice to judge rather than to know is the cause of the loss of peace. Judgment is the process on which perception but not knowledge rests. I have discussed this before in terms of selectivity of perception, pointing out that evaluation is its obvious prerequisite. Judgment always involves rejection. It never emphasizes only the positive aspects of what is judged, whether in you or in others. What has been perceived and rejected, or judged and found wanting, remains in your mind because it has been perceived. One of the illusions from which you suffer is the belief that what you judged against has no effect.

This cannot be true unless you also believe that what you judged against does not exist. You evidently do not believe this, or you would not have judged against it. In the end it does not matter whether your judgment is right or wrong. Either way you are placing your belief in the unreal. This cannot be avoided in any type of judgment, because it implies the belief that reality is yours to select from."

Gene: When you judge another, that is a mirror of the judgment of yourself. Judgment always involves condemnation, a good/bad guy, right/wrong situation, in which there is a winner and a loser. What we see in others is what we see in ourselves. Therefore, whatever attribute I see in others is what I see in myself. More importantly, what I want for others is what I will receive in my life. Taking it up to even a higher level, how we judge/view others is how we feel God will view us. The more loving one becomes towards his brothers and sisters, the more loving will be one's experience of God.

CHAPTER 39

Text, page 49: "Devil"

A COURSE IN MIRACLES interpretation: "The "devil" is a frightening concept because he seems to be extremely powerful and extremely active. He is perceived as a force in combat with God, battling Him for possession of His creations. The devil deceives by lies, and builds kingdoms in which everything is in direct opposition to God. Yet he attracts men rather than repels them, and they are willing to "sell" him their souls in return for gifts of no real worth. This makes absolutely no sense. The mind can make the belief in separation very real and very fearful, and this belief is the "devil." It is powerful, active, destructive and clearly in opposition to God, because it literally denies His Fatherhood."

Gene: The devil is any thought we have with our ego. Therefore whether I am angry, fearful, judging, etc., the Course says these feelings keep us from listening to the Voice of God. These thoughts can be called devil thoughts.

CHAPTER 40

Text, page 50: "Forbidden tree" and "Tree of knowledge"

A COURSE IN MIRACLES interpretation: "We have discussed the fall or separation before, but its meaning must be clearly understood. The separation is a system of thought real enough in time, though not in eternity. All beliefs are real to the believer. The fruit of only one tree was "forbidden" in the symbolic garden. But God could not have forbidden it, or it could not have been eaten. If God knows His children, and I assure you that He does, would He have put them in a position where their own destruction was possible? The "forbidden tree" was named the "tree of knowledge." Yet God created knowledge and gave it freely to His creations. The symbolism here has been given many interpretations, but you may be sure that any interpretation that sees either God or His creations as capable of destroying Their Own purpose is in error."

Gene: The "forbidden tree" was named the "tree of knowledge." God only loves us and gives Her Love freely to all Her children. The only thing that can emanate from Love is Love. Therefore God being Love could never put Her children in a situation where they could destroy themselves. The only thing that can emanate from Love is Love. Therefore God being Love could never put Her children in a position where they could experience pain in any form.

CHAPTER 41

Text, page 51: "Branch that bears no fruit."

A COURSE IN MIRACLES interpretation: "The branch that bears no fruit will be cut off and will wither away. Be glad! The light will shine from the true Foundation of life, and your own thought system will stand corrected. You who fear salvation are choosing death. Life and death, light and darkness, knowledge and perception, are irreconcilable."

Gene: Any thought that doesn't bear the fruits of God will have to wither and die. Once we start connecting happiness with God thoughts, we will naturally let the other thoughts slip out of our awareness or die.

CHAPTER 42

Text, page 52: "The Bible says that you should go with a brother twice as far as he asks."

A COURSE IN MIRACLES interpretation: "It certainly does not suggest that you set him back on his journey. Devotion to a brother cannot set you back either. It can lead only to mutual progress. The result of genuine devotion is inspiration, a word which properly understood is the opposite of fatigue. To be fatigued is to be dis-spirited, but to be inspired is to be in spirit. To be egocentric is to be dis-spirited, but to be Self-centered in the right sense is to be inspired or in spirit. The truly inspired are enlightened and cannot abide in darkness."

Gene: To the degree that we are devoted to our brothers and sisters is the exact degree we will be devoted to ourselves. And equally important is the degree we recognize who we are as a child of God. When we are devoted to our brothers and sisters, we feel inspired and enlightened.

CHAPTER 43

Text, page 52: "Be still and know that I am God."

A COURSE IN MIRACLES interpretation: "You can speak from the spirit or from the ego, as you choose. If you speak from spirit you have chosen to "Be still and know that I am God." These words are inspired because they reflect knowledge. If you speak from the ego you are disclaiming knowledge instead of affirming it, and are thus dis-spiriting yourself. Do not embark on useless journeys, because they are indeed in vain. The ego may desire them, but spirit cannot embark on them because it is forever unwilling to depart from its Foundation."

Gene: Only in stillness can one know God. When we are in conflict or when we are judging, our energy vibration is not on the same vibrational frequency as God's. This discord makes it impossible to know God.

CHAPTER 44

Text, page 52: "Useless journey"

A COURSE IN MIRACLE interpretation: "The journey to the cross should be the last "useless journey." Do not dwell upon it, but dismiss it as accomplished. If you can accept it as your own last useless journey, you are also free to join my resurrection. Until you do so your life is indeed wasted. It merely re-enacts the separation, the loss of power, the futile attempts of the ego at reparation, and finally the crucifixion of the body, or death. Such repetitions are endless until they are voluntarily given up."

Gene: Jesus showed us, in an extreme case, that people need not defend themselves. We are to emulate Jesus at a thought level, NOT at the form level. We are not to take up the old rugged cross and follow him, but follow his internal guidance.

CHAPTER 45

Text, page 52: "Clinging to the old rugged cross."

A COURSE IN MIRACLES interpretation: "Do not make the pathetic error of "clinging to the old rugged cross." The only message of the crucifixion is that you can overcome the cross. Until then you are free to crucify yourself as often as you choose. This is not the Gospel I intended to offer you. We have another journey to undertake, and if you will read these lessons carefully they will help prepare you to undertake it."

Gene: Jesus tells us not to follow the old rugged cross/ego thoughts, but instead follow his loving guidance.

CHAPTER 46

Text, page 56: "Elder brother"

A COURSE IN MIRACLES interpretation: "I will substitute for your ego if you wish, but never for your spirit. A father can safely leave a child with an elder brother who has shown himself responsible, but this involves no confusion about the child's origin. The brother can protect the child's body and his ego, but he does not confuse himself with the father because he does this. I can be entrusted with your body and your ego only because this enables you not to be concerned with them, and lets me teach you their unimportance."

Gene: Jesus tells us that we are his equal in that we both come from God. The only difference between us is that Jesus recognizes who he is as a child of God, and we don't. Jesus wants us to look at him as a brother who temporarily knows more than us. As an elder brother can teach a younger sibling how to do certain things, so can Jesus teach us. In his role as elder brother, Jesus, in no way, confuses who the Father is.

CHAPTER 47

Text, page 60: "The Kingdom of Heaven is within you."

A COURSE IN MIRACLES interpretation: "It is hard to understand what "The Kingdom of Heaven is within you" really means. This is because it is not understandable to the ego, which interprets it as if something outside is inside, and this does not mean anything. The word "within" is unnecessary. The Kingdom of Heaven is you. What else but you did the Creator create, and what else but you is His Kingdom? This is the whole message of the Atonement; a message which in its totality transcends the sum of its parts."

Gene: The Course gives this saying a different meaning from what we have heard in New Thought. We are to leave the word "within" out. Now it reads, "The Kingdom of Heaven is you." That has to be true because that is the only thing God created and therefore we are His kingdom.

CHAPTER 48

Text, page 61: "Immeasurable gifts which are for you."

A COURSE IN MIRACLES interpretation: "There is a kind of experience so different from anything the ego can offer that you will never want to cover or hide it again. It is necessary to repeat that your belief in darkness and hiding is why the light cannot enter. The Bible gives many references to the immeasurable gifts which are for you, but for which you must ask. This is not a condition as the ego sets conditions. It is the glorious condition of what you are."

Gene: God gives freely; in fact, She is constantly giving everything to us all the time. It is up to us to recognize these gifts. They are always available for the asking. What blocks them from manifesting in our life are grievances, anger, petty hurts, etc. Any thought that is not love blocks our awareness to the gifts of God.

Text, page 61: "Thou shalt have no other gods before Him."

A COURSE IN MIRACLES interpretation: "No force except your own will is strong enough or worthy enough to guide you. In this you are as free as God, and must remain so forever. Let us ask the Father in my name to keep you mindful of His Love for you and yours for Him. He has never failed to answer this request, because it asks only for what He has already willed. Those who call truly are always answered. Thou shalt have no other gods before Him because there are none."

Gene: There are no other gods before Him because of your total oneness with your Creator. The other gods/ego is not who you truly are. That is why when we listen to our ego we experience pain in our life. We are literally on the wrong channel. Only when we listen to the Voice for God do we truly experience peace. We can listen to other voices but that still doesn't make them real.

CHAPTER 50

Text, page 64: "First Coming"

A COURSE IN MIRACLES interpretation: "The First Coming of Christ is merely another name for the creation, for Christ is the Son of God."

Gene: The first coming is God extending Her love and creating the Christ energy. Because we believe we have separated from God, we feel separate from that energy at times. When we are listening to the Voice for God, we naturally become one with this Christ energy and also become one with what the Course refers to as the Atonement.

CHAPTER 51

Text, page 64: "Second Coming"

A COURSE IN MIRACLES interpretation: "The Second Coming of Christ means nothing more than the end of the ego's rule and the healing of the mind. I was created like you in the First, and I have called you to join with me in the Second. I am in charge of the Second Coming, and my judgment, which is used only for protection, cannot be wrong because it never attacks. Yours may be so distorted that you believe I was mistaken in choosing you. I assure you this is a mistake of your ego. Do not mistake it for humility. Your ego is trying to convince you that it is real and I am not, because if I am real, I am no more real than you are. That knowledge, and I assure you that it is knowledge, means that Christ has come into your mind and healed it."

Gene: The Second Coming is the complete removal of the ego's thought system. Jesus is in charge of this removal process.

CHAPTER 52

Text, page 65: "Raised the dead."

A COURSE IN MIRACLES interpretation: "Your mind will elect to join with mine, and together we are invincible. You and your brother will yet come together in my name, and your sanity will be restored. I raised the dead by knowing that life is an eternal attribute of everything that the living God created. Why do you believe it is harder for me to inspire the dis-spirited or to stabilize the unstable? I do not believe that there is an order of difficulty in miracles; you do. I have called and you will answer. I understand that miracles are natural, because they are expressions of love. My calling you is as natural as your answer, and as inevitable."

Gene: When the Course uses the word "dead," it is very seldom referring to the way we normally use the word. When we are listening to our ego, we are having "dead" thoughts. What Jesus is saying is that he raised his ego thoughts to a level where they were removed from his mind. Then and only then are you truly alive.

He further explains to us there is no order of difficulties in miracles, which means there are no big or little "dead" thoughts, but simply thoughts we have with the ego. All ego thoughts have one purpose, and that is to keep us away from listening to the Voice for God.

CHAPTER 53

Text, page 66: "Seek and ye shall find."

A COURSE IN MIRACLES interpretation: "This is the question that must be asked: "Where can I go for protection?" "Seek and ye shall find" does not mean that you should seek blindly and desperately for something you would not recognize. Meaningful seeking is consciously undertaken, consciously organized and consciously directed. The goal must be formulated clearly and kept in mind. Learning and wanting to learn are inseparable. You learn best when you believe what you are trying to learn is of value to you. However, not everything you may want to learn has lasting value. Indeed, many of the things you want to learn may be chosen because their value will not last."

Gene: The statement should be changed to "meaningful" seeking. Most people seek by default. And by that I mean they look outside. This looking generates a feeling, and this feeling determines what they look for. Meaningful seeing means to look inside, seek that thought which brings us joy and seek only that. We are always seeking for peace, the problem is at times we associate peace with listening to our ego. When we finally realize that peace only comes from God then we truly will be seeking meaningfully.

CHAPTER 54

Text, page 70: "Praise God"

A COURSE IN MIRACLES interpretation: "The Bible repeatedly states that you should praise God. This hardly means that you should tell Him how wonderful he is. He has no ego with which to accept such praise, and no perception with which to judge it. But unless you take your part in the creation, His joy is not complete because yours is incomplete. And this He does know. He knows it in His Own Being and its experience of His Son's experience. The constant going out of His Love is blocked when His channels are closed."

Gene: God doesn't need our praise because She has no ego that needs to be stroked. We should give thanks for Her Love and guidance which automatically connects us to our Source. Gratitude is an aspect of Love and they can never be separate.

CHAPTER 55

Text, page 73: "May the mind be in you that was also in Christ Jesus."

A COURSE IN MIRACLES interpretation: "I have said already that I can reach up and bring the Holy Spirit down to you, but I can bring Him to you only at your own invitation. The Holy Spirit is in your right mind, as He was in mine. The Bible says, "May the mind be in you that was also in Christ Jesus," and uses this as a blessing. It is the blessing of miracle-mindedness. It asks that you may think as I thought, joining with me in Christ thinking."

Gene: The thoughts that were and are in Jesus is that of the Holy Spirit/God. They are always there; but our mind has the option of listening to another voice, noted in the Course as the ego. It is up to us to choose the Holy Spirit, and this is accomplished when we no longer see any value in listening to the ego.

CHAPTER 56

Text, page 74: "If I go I will send you another Comforter and he will abide with you."

A COURSE IN MIRACLES interpretation: "I myself said, "If I go I will send you another Comforter and he will abide with you." His symbolic function makes the Holy Spirit difficult to understand, because symbolism is open to different interpretations. As a man and also one of God's creations, my right thinking, which came from the Holy Spirit or the Universal Inspiration, taught me first and foremost that this Inspiration is for all. I could not have It myself without knowing this. The word "know" is proper in this context, because the Holy Spirit is so close to knowledge that He calls it forth; or better, allows it to come."

Gene: The Comforter he was referring to, of course, is the Holy Spirit. We are never without this Voice that is lovingly and gently guiding us.

CHAPTER 57

Text, page 77: "All power in Heaven and earth."

A COURSE IN MIRACLES interpretation: "My mind will always be like yours, because we were created as equals. It was only my decision that gave me all power in Heaven and earth. My only gift to you is to help you make the same decision. This decision is the choice to share it, because the decision itself is the decision to share. It is made by giving, and is therefore the one choice that resembles true creation."

Gene: Jesus' thought process does give him dominion over everything because he shares only his thoughts with God. He tells us we are his equal and will show us how to listen to only one voice and become co-creators with God; thereby recognizing we have complete dominion over every external circumstance.

CHAPTER 58

Text, page 77: "Model for learning"

A COURSE IN MIRACLES interpretation: "I am your model for decision. By deciding for God I showed you that this decision can be made, and that you can make it."

Gene: We are to model Jesus at a thought level, not the form level. I'm sure everyone has heard the saying "What would Jesus do?" Well, Jesus would ask God what to do. Technically that is not correct, because he has no ego and is part of the Holy Trinity, so that is the only Voice he is capable of hearing. To ask implies one not knowing. Jesus is constantly in touch with the Knowing.

What that means for us is that in each and every circumstance, we are to ask Jesus what to do. Again, don't try to picture what he would do, ask him. He might tell you to do something different each time for the same ongoing problem. That is because we can only hear the amount of love that we will let in at any given time.

CHAPTER 59

Text, page 77: "My yoke is easy and my burden light."

A COURSE IN MIRACLES interpretation: "When you are tempted by the wrong voice, call on me to remind you how to heal by sharing my decision and making it stronger. As we share this goal, we increase its power to attract the whole Sonship, and to bring it back into the oneness in which it was created. Remember that "yoke" means "join together," and "burden" means "message." Let us restate "My yoke is easy and my burden light" in this way; "Let us join together, for my message is light."

Gene: When we turn our thoughts to Jesus everything becomes easy because of our united power. In this joining we are in the "light."

CHAPTER 60

Text, page 82: "Turning the other cheek."

A COURSE IN MIRACLES interpretation: "I heard one Voice because I understood that I could not atone for myself alone. Listening to one Voice implies the decision to share It in order to hear It myself. The Mind that was in me is still irresistibly drawn to every mind created by God, because God's Wholeness is still irresistibly drawn to every mind created by God, because God's Wholeness is the Wholeness of His Son. You cannot be hurt, and do not want to show your brother anything except your wholeness. Show him that he cannot hurt you and hold nothing against him, or you hold it against yourself. This is the meaning of "turning the other cheek.""

Gene: We turn from listening to the ego's view of any given situation to the Holy Spirit's view. In this energy field no one can hurt you, and you will be able to show love to your brothers and sisters regardless of external happenings.

CHAPTER 61

Text, page 87: "As you sow shall ye reap."

A COURSE IN MIRACLES interpretation: "He interprets to mean what you consider worth cultivating you will cultivate in yourself. Your judgment of what is worthy makes it worthy for you."

Gene: Whatever we put our attention on, we will manifest in our lives. The world is not good or bad, but simply an outside picture of an inward thought.

CHAPTER 62

Text, page 87: "Vengeance is mine, sayeth the Lord."

A COURSE IN MIRACLES interpretation: "Is easily reinterpreted if you remember that ideas increase only by being shared. The statement emphasizes that vengeance cannot be shared. Give it therefore to the Holy Spirit, Who will undo it in you because it does not belong in your mind, which is part of God."

Gene: Once again the Course gives us a completely different view of one of the more blood-stained interpretations. All this is saying is give/share with God your thoughts that contain any trace of vengeance.

CHAPTER 63

Text, page 87: "I will visit the sins of the fathers unto the third and fourth generation."

A COURSE IN MIRACLES interpretation: "As interpreted by the ego, this is particularly vicious. It becomes merely an attempt to guarantee the ego's own survival. To the Holy Spirit, the statement means that in later generations He can still reinterpret what former generations had misunderstood, and thus release the thoughts from the ability to produce fear."

Gene: This is most definitely a frightening statement the way it has been depicted in our churches. The Course's view means that the Holy Spirit can reinterpret the errors of former generations and thus release all the consequences that any misunderstood thought produced by prior generations.

CHAPTER 64

Text, page 87: "The wicked shall perish."

A COURSE IN MIRACLES interpretation: "This becomes a statement of Atonement, if the word "perish" is understood as "be undone." Every loveless thought must be undone, a word the ego cannot even understand. To the ego, to be undone means to be destroyed. The ego will not be destroyed because it is part of your thought, but because it is uncreative and therefore unsharing, it will be reinterpreted to release you from fear. The part of your mind that you have given to the ego will merely return to the Kingdom, where your whole mind belongs. You can delay the completion of the kingdom, but you cannot introduce the concept of fear into it."

Gene: "Perish" means to be undone or removed. What will perish is the way we look at things. We will no longer view things with our ego but through the eyes of Love.

CHAPTER 65

Text, page 88: "I am come as a light into the world."

A COURSE IN MIRACLES interpretation: "When I said "I am come as a light into the world," I meant that I came to share the light with you. Remember my reference to I came to share the light with you. Remember my reference to the ego's dark glass, and remember also that I said, "Do not look there." It is still true that where you look to find yourself is up to you. Your patience with your brother is your patience with yourself. Is not a child of God worth patience? I have shown you infinite patience because my will is that of our Father, from Whom I learned of infinite patience. His Voice was in me as It is in you, speaking for patience towards the Sonship in the Name of its Creator."

Gene: Jesus came as a light into the world to share it with us. Since we are one with him, that light is always present. He is constantly reminding us where to look, and his patience is infinite.

CHAPTER 66

Text, page 88: "Thine is the Kingdom."

A COURSE IN MIRACLES interpretation: "You need not fear the Higher Court will condemn you. It will merely dismiss the case against you. There can be no case against a child of God, and every witness to guilt in God's creations is bearing false witness to God Himself. Appeal everything you believe gladly to God's Own Higher Court, because it speaks for Him and therefore speaks truly. The case may be fool-proof, but it is not God-proof. The Holy Spirt will not hear it, because He can only witness truly. His verdict will always be "thine is the Kingdom," because He was given to you to remind you of what you are."

Gene: "Thine is the Kingdom" means the Voice for God was given us to always remind us of who we are as a child of God. God's Love always overrules the decisions of the ego.

CHAPTER 67

Text, page 89: "They have not moved mountains."

A COURSE IN MIRACLES interpretation: Refer to Chapter 68 for quote.

Gene: Mountains are simply "big" ego thoughts. This also applies to the word "dead." One can only move the mountains of ego thoughts when they are removed in the healer's mind. Fortunately this does not mean that we have to have all our ego thoughts removed. What this means is we have to have them removed for an instant; and an instant is sufficient; healing waits not on time.

CHAPTER 68

Text, page 89: "Raised the dead."

A COURSE IN MIRACLES interpretation: "There have been many healers who did not heal themselves. They have not moved mountains by their faith because their faith was not whole. Some of them have healed the sick at times, but they have not raised the dead. Unless the healer heals himself, he cannot believe that there is no order of difficulty in miracles. He has not learned that every mind God created is equally worthy of being healed because God created it whole. He asks you only for what He gave, knowing that this giving will heal you. Sanity is wholeness, and the sanity of your brothers is yours."

Gene: Raising the dead simply means to raise our ego thoughts to the level of Christ Consciousness. In this manner, they can be removed; because at this frequency there are no big, mountainous thoughts, only loving thoughts.

CHAPTER 69

Text, page 89: "One mind"

A COURSE IN MIRACLES interpretation: "Why should you listen to the endless insane calls you think are made upon you, when you can know the Voice for God is in you? God commended His Spirit to you, and asks that you commend yours to Him. He wills to keep it in perfect peace, because you are of one mind and spirit with Him. Excluding yourself from the Atonement is the ego's last-ditch defense of its own existence. It reflects both the ego's need to separate, and our willingness to side with its separateness. This willingness means that you do not want to be healed."

Gene: To be of one mind is to listen only to the part of our mind that is connected to God. That truly is the only part that is real.

CHAPTER 70

Text, page 91: "Crucifixion"

A COURSE IN MIRACLES interpretation: "For learning purposes, let us consider the crucifixion again. I did not dwell on it before because of the fearful connotations you may associate with it. The only emphasis laid upon it so far has been that it was not a form of punishment. Nothing, however, can be explained in negative terms only. There is a positive interpretation of the crucifixion that is wholly devoid of fear, and therefore wholly benign in what it teaches, if it is properly understood.

The crucifixion is nothing more than an extreme example. Its value, like the value of any teaching device, lies solely in the kind of learning it facilitates. It can be, and has been misunderstood. This is only because the fearful are apt to perceive fearfully. I have already told you that you can always call on me to share my decision, and thus make it stronger. I have also told you that the crucifixion was the last useless journey the Sonship need take, and that it represents release from fear to anyone who understand it.

While I emphasized only the resurrection before, the purpose of the crucifixion and how it actually led to the resurrection was not clarified then. Nevertheless, it has a definite contribution to make in your own life, and if you will consider it without fear, it will help you understand your own role as a teacher. You have probably reacted for years as if you were being crucified. This is a marked tendency of the separated, who always refuse to consider what they have done to themselves. Projection means anger, fosters assault, and assault promotes fear. The real meaning of the crucifixion lies in the apparent intensity of the assault of some of the Sons of God upon another. This, of course, is impossible, and must be fully understood as impossible. Otherwise, I cannot serve as a model for learning.

Assault can ultimately be made only on the body. There is little doubt that one body can assault another, and even destroy it. Yet if destruction itself is impossible, anything that is destructible cannot be real. Its destruction, therefore, does not justify anger. To the extent to which you believe that it does, you are accepting false premises and teaching them to others. The message of the crucifixion was intended to teach was that it is not necessary to perceive any form of assault in persecution, because you cannot be persecuted. If you respond with anger, you must be equating yourself with the destructible and are therefore regarding yourself insanely."

Gene: The crucifixion is another frightening tool the church uses to make people feel guilty and get them to do what they want. Jesus used the crucifixion as a teaching aid to show us in an extreme case that one need not defend themselves. We act daily as though we have been crucified only because we feel that crucifying others is in our own best interest. Jesus shows us that one body can crucify another; but since we are not a body, he could not have been crucified.

CHAPTER 71

A COURSE IN MIRACLES interpretation: See Chapter 73 for quote.

Gene: The resurrection is the reawakening from the dream that your ego can help you find the peace we all are so desperately seeking. Then we will recognize who we are as a child of God and naturally want to share that love with all our brother and sisters.

CHAPTER 72

Text, page 93: "The way, the truth and the light."

A COURSE IN MIRACLES interpretation: See Chapter 73 for quote.

Gene: When Jesus listened to God, he knew the way, the truth, and the light. He did what all of us are capable of doing. He is not the only way, but the energy of Love is the only way. So, when we follow the energy of Love, we, too, are the way, the truth, and the light.

CHAPTER 73

Text, page 93: "Agony in the garden."

A COURSE IN MIRACLES interpretation: "Your resurrection is your reawakening. I am the model for rebirth, but rebirth itself is merely the dawning on your mind of what is already in it. God placed it there Himself, and so it is true forever. I believed in it, and therefore accepted it as true for me. Help me to teach it to our brothers in the name of the Kingdom of God, but first believe that it is true for you, or you will teach amiss. My brothers slept during the so-called "agony in the garden," but I could not be angry with them because I knew I could not be abandoned.

I am sorry when my brothers do not share my decision to hear only one Voice, because it weakens them as teachers and as learners. Yet I know they cannot really betray themselves or me, and that it is still on them that I must build my church. There is no choice in this, because only you can be the foundation of God's church. A church is where an altar is, and the presence of the altar is what makes the church holy. A church that does not inspire love has a hidden altar that is not serving the purpose for which God intended it. I must found His church on you, because those who accept me as a model are literally my disciples. Disciples are followers, and if the model they follow has chosen to save them pain in all respects, they are unwise not to follow him.

I elected, for your sake and mine, to demonstrate that the most outrageous assault, as judged by the ego, does not matter. As the world judges these things, but not as God knows them, I was betrayed, abandoned, beaten, torn, and finally killed. It was clear that this was only because of the projection of others unto me, since I had not harmed any-one and had healed many.

We are still equal as learners, although we do not need to have equal experiences. The Holy Spirit is glad when you can learn from mine, and be reawakened by them. That is their only purpose, and that is the only way in which I can be perceived as the way, the truth and the life. When you hear only one Voice you are never called on to sacrifice. On the contrary, by being able to hear the Holy Spirit in oth-ers you can learn from their experiences, and can gain from them without experiencing them directly yourself. That is because the Holy Spirit is one, and anyone who listens is inevitably led to demonstrate His way for all.

You are not persecuted, nor was I. You are not asked to repeat my experiences because the Holy Spirit, Whom we share, makes this unnecessary. To use my experiences con-structively, however, you must still follow my example in how to perceive them. My brothers and yours are constantly engaged in justifying the unjustifiable. My one lesson, which I must teach as I learned it, is that no perception that is out of accord with the judgment of the Holy Spirit can be justified. I undertook to show this was true in an extreme case, merely because it would serve as a good teaching aid to those whose temptation to give in to anger and assault would not be so extreme. I will with God that none of His Sons should suffer.

The crucifixion cannot be shared because it is the symbol of projection, but the resurrection is the symbol of sharing because the reawakening of every Son of God is necessary to enable the Sonship to know its Wholeness. The message of the crucifixion is perfectly clear:

"Teach only love, for that is what you are."

Gene: This is another example of the many things that Jesus supposedly said that he simply says did not occur He could not have experienced anger towards any of his brothers who slept because he knew he could not have been abandoned.

CHAPTER 74

Text, page 94: "Wrath of God."

A COURSE IN MIRACLES interpretation: "If you interpret the crucifixion in any other way, you are using it as a weapon for assault rather than a call for peace for which it was intended. The Apostles often misunderstood it, and for the same reason that anyone misunderstands it. Their own imperfect love made them vulnerable to projection, and out of their own fear they spoke of the "wrath of God" as His retaliatory weapon. Nor could they speak of the crucifixion entirely without anger, because their sense of guilt had made them angry."

Gene: Jesus is simply telling us that the "wrath of God" is impossible. It is one way man justifies his inhumanity towards his fellow brothers and sisters. The only thing that can come from God is Love because that is the only thing God is.

Text, page 95: "I come not to bring peace but a sword."

A COURSE IN MIRACLES interpretation: See Chapter 77 for quote.

Gene: Jesus tell us that he didn't say "I come not to bring peace but a sword."

CHAPTER 76

Text, page 95: "Punishment of Judas."

A COURSE IN MIRACLES interpretation: See Chapter 77 for quote.

Gene: The punishment of Judas. Again, another example of where the Bible has Jesus quoting something that he denies in A COURSE IN MIRACLES when he says, "I could not have said that because Judas was my brother walking back to God."

CHAPTER 77

Text, page 95: "Betrayest thou the Son of man with a kiss?"

A COURSE IN MIRACLES interpretation: "These are some of the examples of upside-down thinking in the New Testament, although its gospel is really only the message of love. If the Apostles had not felt guilty, they never could have quoted me as saying, "I come not to bring peace but a sword." This is clearly the opposite of everything I taught. Nor could they have really understood me. I could not have said, "Betrayest thou the Son of man with a kiss?" unless I believed in betrayal. The whole message of the crucifixion was simply that I did not. The "punishment" I was said to have called forth upon Judas was a similar mistake. Judas was my brother and a Son of God, as much a part of the Sonship as myself. Was it likely that I would condemn him when I was ready to demonstrate that condemnation is impossible?"

Gene: Once again Jesus simply says he didn't say that.

CHAPTER 78

Text, page 95: "They (Apostles) would understand later"

A COURSE IN MIRACLES interpretation: "As you read the teachings of the Apostles, remember that I told them myself that there was much they would understand later, because they were not wholly ready to follow me at the time. I do not want you to allow any fear to enter into the thought system toward which I am guiding you. I do not call for martyrs but for teachers."

Gene: Jesus simply said they weren't ready to hear parts of his message because at the time they still held out hope that he was the Messiah.

CHAPTER 79

Text, page 106: "Many thought I was attacking them, even though it was apparent I was not."

A COURSE IN MIRACLES interpretation: "All who believe in separation have a basic fear of retaliation and abandonment. They believe in attack and rejection, so that is what they perceive and teach and learn. These insane ideas are clearly the result of dissociation and projection. What you teach you are, but it is quite apparent that you can teach wrongly, and can therefore teach yourself wrong. Many thought I was attacking them, even though it was apparent I was not. An insane learner learns strange lessons. What you must recognize is that when you do not share a thought system, you are weakening it. Those who believe in it therefore perceive this as an attack on them. This is because everyone identifies himself with his thought system, and every thought system centers on what you believe you are. If the center of the thought system is true, only truth extends from it. But if a lie is at its center, only deception proceeds from it."

Gene: What Jesus was trying to get across to us over two thousand years ago was a threat to the establishment at the time. To those people, he was perceived as an enemy of the state and had to be removed. He never attacked or judged anyone, but simply offered love and healed many.

CHAPTER 80

Text, page 116: "I am with you always."

A COURSE IN MIRACLES interpretation: "When I said "I am with you always," I meant it literally. I am not absent to anyone in any situation. Because I am always with you, you are the way the truth and the life. You did not make this power, any more than I did. It was created to be shared, and therefore cannot be meaningfully perceived as belonging to anyone at the expense of another. Such a perception makes it meaningless by eliminating or overlooking its real and only meaning."

Gene: As he told us earlier, one of the lessons one needed to learn from the crucifixion was that even though the body may be destroyed, communication remains unbroken. He is still there for us now as much as he was two thousand years ago.

CHAPTER 81

Text, page 119: "Seek ye first the Kingdom of Heaven."

A COURSE IN MIRACLES interpretation: "Seek ye first the kingdom of Heaven, because that is where the laws of God operate truly, and they can operate only truly because they are the laws of truth. But seek this only, because you can find nothing else. There is nothing else. God is All in all in a very literal sense."

Gene: Jesus tells us here that the laws of truth are the only thing that will make us happy. Therefore, seeking for guidance from the Holy Spirit is truly the only thing that will make us happy. The trouble most people have is that they believe that the Holy Spirit will deprive them of the various pleasures of the world. The Holy Spirit will only enhance everything that we desire and everything that we do. We enjoy a massage more, food tastes delightful, sex is so much more satisfying, etc.

All the Holy Spirit is asking is that we invite Him to join us with our desires and interactions with others.

CHAPTER 82

Text, page 141: "All power and glory are yours because the Kingdom is His."

A COURSE IN MIRACLES interpretation: "This is what I meant: The Will of God is without limit, and all power and glory lie with it. It is boundless in strength and in love and in peace. It has no boundaries because its extension is unlimited, and it encompasses all things because it created all things. By creating all things, it made them part of itself. Because your Creator creates only like Himself, you are like Him. You are part of Him Who is all power and glory, and are therefore as unlimited as He is."

Gene: When you unite your will with God's you have all power because true unlimited power comes from God. God's Love makes all things; therefore, you are one with everything.

CHAPTER 83

Text, page 141: "Glory to God in the highest."

A COURSE IN MIRACLES interpretation: See Chapter 84 for quote.

Gene: This statement doesn't mean we need to tell God how wonderful He is. God is absent of ego and needs not the attention of praise. He is all powerful and all knowing and we are one with that power.

CHAPTER 84

Text, page 141: "Ask and it is given."

A COURSE IN MIRACLES interpretation: "Glory to God in the highest, and to you because He has so willed. Ask and it shall be given you, because it has already been given. Ask for light and learn that you are light. If you want understanding and enlightenment you will learn it, because your decision to learn it is the decision to listen to the Teacher Who knows of light, and can therefore teach it to you. There is no limit on your learning because there is no limit on your mind. There is no limit on His teaching because He was created to teach. Understanding His function perfectly He fulfills it perfectly, because that is His joy and yours."

Gene: Every thought we have is an asking, and asking has to be answered. Is the question coming from the ego or the Holy Spirit, the answering is inevitable. When we ask to see only love that is all we will see and God will have to answer. If we ask for punishment of oneself or another, God cannot grant a request He knows nothing of. It will be answered because of the asking but the answer will come from the voice of fear. This voice believes that you, your brothers and sisters are all deserving of punishment and lack because all of you have sinned.

Text, page 144: "I am come as a light into a world."

A COURSE IN MIRACLES interpretation: See Chapter 88 for quote.

Gene: Jesus states "I am come as a light into a world" because light is associated with listening to the Voice for God. Since that is the only Voice Jesus listened to, he was a light into a world where darkness seems to exist.

CHAPTER 86

**Text, page 144: "I am with you always,
even unto the end of the world."**

A COURSE IN MIRACLES interpretation: See Chapter
88 for quote.

Gene: "I am with you always, even unto the end of the
world." As he stated earlier, he is as accessible to us now
as he was two thousand years ago. He is the light/love that
shines away the darkness of our ego thoughts.

CHAPTER 87

Text, page 144: "I have overcome the world."

A COURSE IN MIRACLES interpretation: See Chapter 88 for quote.

Gene: "I have overcome the world." This refers to Jesus having completely overcome his ego thought system.

CHAPTER 88

Text, page 144: "Do this in remembrance of me."

A COURSE IN MIRACLES interpretation: "I am come as a light into a world that does deny itself everything. It does this simply by dissociating itself from everything. It is therefore an illusion of isolation, maintained by fear of the same loneliness that is its illusion. I said that I am with you always, even unto the end of the world. That is why I am the light of the world. If I am with you in the loneliness of the world, the loneliness is gone. You cannot maintain the illusion of loneliness if you are not alone. My purpose, then, is still to overcome the world. I do not attack it, but my light must dispel it because of what it is. The light becomes ours, and you cannot abide in darkness any more than darkness can abide wherever you go. The remembrance of me is the remembrance of yourself, and of Him Who sent me to you.

You were in darkness until God's Will was done completely by any part of the Sonship. When this was done, it was perfectly accomplished by all. How else could it be perfectly accomplished? My mission was simply to unite the will of the Sonship with the Will of the Father by being aware of the Father's Will myself. This is the awareness I came to give you, and your problem in accepting it is the problem of this world. Dispelling it is salvation, and in this sense I am the salvation of the world. The world must therefore despise and reject me, because the world is the belief that love is impossible. If you will accept the fact that I am with you, you are denying the world and accepting God. My will is His, and your decision to hear me is the decision to hear His Voice and abide in His Will. As God sent me to you so will I send you to others. And I will go to them with you, so we can teach them peace and union."

Gene: How Jesus wants us to remember him is to listen to his guidance as he gently and lovingly removes the veil/ego thoughts that blocks us from experiencing his eternal love.

CHAPTER 89

Text, page 146: "The Holy Trinity"

A COURSE IN MIRACLES interpretation: "Freedom is the only gift you can offer to God's Sons, being an acknowledgment of what they are and what He is. Freedom is creation, because it is love. Whom you seek to imprison you do not love. Therefore, when you seek to imprison anyone, including yourself, you do not love him and you cannot identify with him. When you imprison yourself you are losing sight of your true identification with me and with the Father. It cannot be with One and not the Other. If you are part of One you must be part of the Other, because they are One. The Holy Trinity is holy because It is One. If you exclude yourself from this union, you are perceiving the Holy Trinity as separated. You must be included in It, because It is everything. Unless you take your place in It and fulfill your function as part of It, the Holy Trinity is as bereft as you are. No part of It can be imprisoned if Its truth is to be known."

Gene: The Holy Trinity is the union of myself, all our brothers and sisters, the Holy Spirit and God. When I said, in the previous sentence, "myself, all our brothers and sisters," that included our elder brother, Jesus. If we deny anyone we denied our union with the Holy Trinity and any and all its parts.

Text, page 148: "Prodigal son."

A COURSE IN MIRACLES interpretation: "Listen to the story of the prodigal son, and learn what God's treasure is and yours: This son of a loving father left his home and thought he had squandered everything for nothing of any value, although he had not understood its worthlessness at the time. He was ashamed to return to his father, because he thought he had hurt him. Yet when he came home the father welcomed him with joy, because the son himself was his father's treasure. He wanted nothing else."

Gene: God wants only His Son because His Son is the only thing he created. We all make up the Son of God. This statement is not exclusively referring to Jesus, but definitely includes Jesus, as it includes each and everyone of us. God created us in His image and likeness, and we are His only treasure.

CHAPTER 91

Text, page 152: "The Word was made flesh."

A COURSE IN MIRACLE interpretation: "The Bible says, "The Word (or thought) was made flesh." Strictly speaking this is impossible, since it seems to involve the translation of one order of reality into another. Different orders of reality merely appear to exist, just as different orders of miracles do. Thought cannot be made into flesh except by belief, since thought is not physical. Yet thought is communication, for which the body can be used. This is the only natural use to which it can be put. To use the body unnaturally is to lose sight of the Holy Spirit's purpose, and thus to confuse the goal of His curriculum."

Gene: Everything in flesh was first a thought. Nothing exists on our planet that was not first a thought in the mind of a child of God.

CHAPTER 92

Text, page 159: "Heal in my name."

A COURSE IN MIRACLES interpretation: "To be perfect, and to heal all errors, to take no thought of the body as separate and to accomplish all things in my name."

Gene: The only way to be perfect is to connect with our Divine source as Jesus did. From that point we are perfect, can heal all errors in ourselves as well as others in Jesus's name.

CHAPTER 93

Text, page 159: "God's Son"

A COURSE IN MIRACLES interpretation: "The Bible enjoins you to be perfect, to heal all errors, to take no thought of the body as separate and to accomplish all things in my name. This is not my name alone, for ours is a shared identification. The Name of God's Son is one, and you are enjoined to do the works of love because we share this Oneness. Our minds are whole because they are one. If you are sick you are withdrawing from me. Yet you cannot withdraw from me alone. You can only withdraw from yourself and me."

Gene: When Jesus refers to God's Son in A COURSE IN MIRACLES, it is never referring exclusively to Jesus. We all make up the embodiment of God's Son.

CHAPTER 94

Text, page 160: "Will of God."

A COURSE IN MIRACLES interpretation: "Fear of the Will of God is one of the strangest beliefs the human mind has ever made. It could not possibly have occurred unless the mind were already profoundly split, making it possible for it to be afraid of what it really is. Reality cannot "threaten" anything except illusions, since reality can only uphold truth. The very fact that the Will of God, which is what you are, is perceived as fearful, demonstrates that you are afraid of what you are. It is not, then, the Will of God of which you are afraid, but yours."

Gene: The reason for the great fear of God is because, as the Course tells us, "no one can conceive of his Creator as unlike himself." Therefore, if I have an ego, I will have to project the way I am onto God and perceive a God like myself. That is why the Course wants you to love yourself and your brothers and sisters. To the degree that I love them will be the degree that I experience God's Love for me. That's why the more loving I become, the more of a loving God I will perceive in my life. Another way of looking at the previous sentence would be to say, "to the degree I can love my brothers and sisters is to the degree I will allow the Love of God into my life."

CHAPTER 95

Text, page 164: "All prayer is answered."

A COURSE IN MIRACLES interpretation: "The Bible emphasizes that all prayer is answered, and this is indeed true. The very fact that the Holy Spirit has been asked for anything will ensure a response. Yet it is equally certain that no response given by Him will ever be one that would increase fear. It is possible that His answer will not be heard. It is impossible, however, that it will be lost. There are many answers you have already received but have not yet heard. I assure you that they are waiting for you."

Gene: Every thought is a prayer. That's why the Course tells us that every thought produces something in our life. Prayers that emanate from one's ego will not be answered by the Voice for God because the Holy Spirit cannot hear them. Those types of prayers are on a different frequency which makes the answering impossible. How can the Voice for Love answer a request for the punishment of oneself or another?

CHAPTER 96

Text, page 170: "Last Judgment"

A COURSE IN MIRACLES interpretation: See Chapter 97 for quote.

Gene: The "Last Judgment" is the final removal of any residual ego thoughts we have left. Welcome the last judgment. It is not where God deals out punishment, but finally, our acceptance of our complete connection to God.

CHAPTER 97

Text, page 170: "Second Coming"

A COURSE IN MIRACLES interpretation: "The ego literally lives on borrowed time, and its days are numbered. Do not fear the Last Judgment, but welcome it and do not wait, for the ego's time is "borrowed" from your eternity. This is the Second Coming that was made for you as the First was created. The Second Coming is merely the return of sense. Can this possibly be fearful?

The impossible can happen only in fantasy. When you search for reality in fantasies you will not find it. The symbols of fantasy are of the ego, and of these you will find many. But do not look for meaning in them. They have no more meaning than the fantasies into which they are woven. Fairy tales can be pleasant or fearful, but no one calls them true. Yet when reality dawns, the fantasies are gone. Reality has not gone in the meanwhile. The Second Coming is the awareness of reality, not its return."

Gene: The Second Coming has nothing to do with Jesus returning in flesh to the planet as some religions would have us believe. The Second Coming is the complete removal of our ego thoughts. At this point we return to our total awareness of our oneness with our Creator.

CHAPTER 98

Text, page 172: "Let there be light."

A COURSE IN MIRACLES interpretation: "When God said, "Let there be light," there was light. Can you find light by analyzing darkness, as the psychotherapist does, or like the theologian, by acknowledging darkness in yourself and looking for a distant light to remove it, while emphasizing the distance? Healing is not mysterious. Nothing will change unless it is understood, since light is understanding.

A therapist does not heal; he lets healing be. He can point to darkness but he cannot bring light of himself, for light is not of him. Yet, being for him, it must also be for his patient. The Holy Spirit is the only Therapist. He makes healing clear in any situation in which He is the Guide. You can only let Him fulfill His function. He needs no help for this. He will tell you exactly what to do to help anyone He sends to you for help, and will speak to him through you if you do not interfere. Remember that you choose the guide for helping, and the wrong choice will not help. But remember also that the right one will. Trust Him, for help is His function, and He is of God."

Gene: Light is synonymous with listening to the Voice for God. Darkness is synonymous with listening to the ego's voice. We cannot figure out what is best for us by studying in darkness, but only by being in light.

CHAPTER 99

Text, page 185: "My peace I give unto you."

A COURSE IN MIRACLES interpretation: "When I said, "My peace I give unto you," I meant it. Peace comes from God through me to you. It is for you although you may not ask for it."

Gene: Jesus gives us his peace because it is its natural expression to extend itself. Love has to go forth from itself. Jesus's love went forth and attached itself to our love, and helps us recognize our divine nature.

CHAPTER 100

Text, page 186: "Jealous God"

A COURSE IN MIRACLES interpretation: "I do not bring God's message with deception, and you will learn this as you learn that you always receive as much as you accept. You could accept peace now for everyone, and offer them perfect freedom from all illusions because you heard His Voice. But have no other gods before Him or you will not hear. God is not jealous of the gods you make, but you are. You would save them and serve them, because you are projecting onto them the fearful fact that you made them to replace God. Yet when they seem to speak to you, remember that nothing can replace God, and whatever replacements you have attempted are nothing."

Gene: A jealous God is impossible because what is omnipresent has everything. This loving God has to give because that is Its nature.

CHAPTER 101

Text, page 190: "Of yourself you can do nothing."

A COURSE IN MIRACLES interpretation: Refer to chapter 102 for quote.

Gene: Of myself I can do nothing that will bring me peace. I can do many different things with my ego, but none will generate the emotion of peace my heart so desperately desires. The act of doing something only applies to the giving over of our fearful thoughts to the Holy Spirit. With no fearful thoughts the Voice for God can now direct us. Then we can experience the peace Jesus desperately wants us to experience.

CHAPTER 102

Text, page 190: "You need be troubled over nothing."

A COURSE IN MIRACLES interpretation: "I said before that of yourself you can do nothing, but you are not of yourself. If you were, what you have made would be true, and you could never escape. It is because you did not make yourself that you need be troubled over nothing. Your gods are nothing, because your Father did not create them. You cannot make creators who are unlike your Creator, any more than He could have created a Son who was unlike Him."

Gene: What Jesus means "of yourself" is that to listen to the ego is to be alone. When we unite with the Holy Spirit we are never alone, and this and only this, is our true Self. This Self knows what we have need of, and will gently guide us in fulfilling our desires.

CHAPTER 103

Text, page 200: "Place no other gods before Him."

A COURSE IN MIRACLES interpretation: "The children of light cannot abide in darkness, for darkness is not in them. Do not be deceived by the dark comforters, and never let them enter the mind of God's Son, for they have no place in His temple. When you are tempted to deny Him remember that there are no other gods to place before Him, and accept His Will for you in peace. For you cannot accept it otherwise."

Gene: What is meant here is that we shouldn't listen to the ego, which is a false idol we employ as a replacement for God. If we do listen to the other voice, it simply will not bring us the peace we think it will. God is not a jealous God and will not punish us for listening to this voice, because God is simply Love and knows not of punishment. When we listen to other gods/voices of the dead, we are aligning our thoughts with future effects that will not bring us the true peace we all desire.

CHAPTER 104

Text, page 208: "I am your resurrection and your life."

A COURSE IN MIRACLES interpretation: "I am your resurrection and your life. You live in me because you live in God. And everyone lives in you, as you live in everyone."

Gene: Resurrection means listening to the Voice for God. When we listen to Jesus, we are listening to this Love station. In listening to this station we now have resurrected/changed our life. Our old perceptual view of the purpose we had given the world will no longer serve us.

Text, page 210: "New Heaven and a new earth."

A COURSE IN MIRACLES interpretation: "The Bible speaks of a new Heaven and a new earth, yet this cannot be literally true, for the eternal are not re-created. To perceive anew is merely to perceive again, implying that before, or in the interval between, you were not perceiving at all. What, then, is the world that awaits your perception when you see it?

The loving thoughts his mind perceives in this world are the world's only reality."

Gene: When we change from our old view of the world to a new more loving view of the world, we literally see it differently. Therefore, what we see is new. But this "new" was always there; we couldn't see it at the time because of old thought patterns that blocked our sight.

CHAPTER 106

Text, page 211: "Become as little children."

A COURSE IN MIRACLES interpretation: "The Bible tells you to become as little children. Little children recognize that they do not understand what they perceive, and so they ask what it means. Do not make the mistake of believing that you understand what you perceive, for its meaning is lost to you. Yet the Holy Spirit has saved its meaning for you, and if you will let Him interpret it, He will restore to you what you have thrown away. Yet while you think you know its meaning, you will see no need to ask it of Him."

Gene: Jesus is telling us that in every circumstance we really don't know what is in our own best interest. From that perspective, we need to humble ourselves and ask, "what is the most loving and kind thing that I can do for myself in this situation?" It is easy for children because they know they don't know; we think we know because of our past life experiences. The barometer for making decisions shouldn't be our past but instead listening to Jesus.

CHAPTER 107

Text, page 212: "The Kingdom of Heaven is within you."

A COURSE IN MIRACLES interpretation: "Beautiful child of God, you are asking only for what I promised you. Believe that the truth is in me, for I know that it is in you. God's Sons have nothing they do not share. Ask for truth of any Son of God, and you have asked it of me. Not one of us but has the answer in him, to give to anyone who asks it of him."

Gene: The Kingdom of Heaven is within each and every one of us. That is why Jesus also tells us in the Bible that "whatever you do to the least of my brothers, you do to me."

The peace of God is first a thought. Thoughts are always internal, and then the internal thought gets projected onto the world, and the world simply mirrors one's loving thoughts.

CHAPTER 108

Text, page 213: "If you perceive offense in a brother pluck the offense from your mind."

A COURSE IN MIRACLES interpretation: "If you perceive the offense in a brother pluck the offense from your mind, for you are offended by Christ and are deceived in Him. Heal in Christ and be not offended by Him, for there is no offense in Him. If what you perceive offends you, you are offended in yourself and are condemning God's Son whom God condemneth not. Let the Holy Spirit remove all offenses of God's Son against himself and perceive no one but through His guidance, for He would save you from all condemnation. Accept His healing power and use it for all He sends you, for He wills to heal the Son of God, in whom He is not deceived."

Gene: Any thought we perceive in another that offends us needs to be removed from our thinking. It is just another way of explaining projection.

CHAPTER 109

Text, page 219: "A little while and you will see me."

A COURSE IN MIRACLES interpretation: "A little while and you will see me, for I am not hidden because you are hiding. I will awaken you as surely as I awakened myself, for I awoke for you. In my resurrection is your release. Our mission is to escape from crucifixion, not from redemption. Trust in my help, for I did not walk alone, and I will walk with you as our Father walked with me. Do you not know that I walked with Him in peace? And does not that mean that peace goes with us on the journey?"

Gene: "A little while" is only the time it takes for you to change your thinking from the ego part of your mind to the Holy Spirit part of you mind. It is only a thought away, so the instant you do that is the instant you will see the effects of the love Jesus has for all of us.

CHAPTER 110

Text, page 220: "Sell all you have and give to the poor and follow me."

A COURSE IN MIRACLES interpretation: "I once asked you to sell all you have and give to the poor and follow me. This is what I meant: If you have no investment in anything in this world, you can teach the poor where their treasure is. The poor are merely those who have invested wrongly, and they are poor indeed! Because they are in need it is given you to help them, since you are among them. Consider how perfectly your lesson would be learned if you were unwilling to share their poverty. For poverty is lack, and there is but one lack since there is but one need."

Gene: What Jesus meant here is to sell/give all your ego investment you have about the world to him so he can have them purified. Any ego thought is a poverty thought. Any thought we have with the Holy Spirit is an abundant thought.

CHAPTER 111

Text, page 222: "God so loved the world that He gave it to His only begotten Son."

A COURSE IN MIRACLES interpretation: "I said before that God so loved the world that He give it to His only begotten Son. God does love the real world, and those who perceive its reality cannot see the world of death."

Gene: God gave the real world, all his Love, to all of us which make up His Son. The real world is a state of mind in which we are totally connected to our Creator. In this state of mind the world is seen as a place of joy and love.

CHAPTER 112

Text, page 233: "Remember that I did not die."

A COURSE IN MIRACLES interpretation: "When you are tempted to yield to the desire for death, remember that I did not die. You will realize that this is true when you look within and see me. Would I have overcome death for myself alone? And would eternal life have been given me of the Father unless He had also given it to you? When you learn to make me manifest, you will never see death. For you will have looked upon the deathless in yourself, and you will see only the eternal as you look out upon a world that cannot die."

Gene: Jesus did not die for two reasons. First, he, as well as you and I, are not a body. Secondly, we can still communicate with him. And when we experience Jesus's love, we will not see death but have eternal life.

CHAPTER 113

Text, page 236: "Adam's sin"

A COURSE IN MIRACLES interpretation: "Adam's sin could have touched no one, had he not believed it was the Father Who drove him out of Paradise. For in that belief the knowledge of the Father was lost, since only those who do not understand Him could believe it. The Atonement is the final lesson he need learn, for it teaches him that, never having sinned, he has no need of salvation."

Gene: Adam's sin technically is impossible. Adam can listen to the ego, and this simply is a mistake. But this mistake does produce results in one's life. Forgiveness is the removal of those false beliefs and its consequences.

CHAPTER 114

Text, page 251: "Born again"

A COURSE IN MIRACLES interpretation: "To be born again is to let the past go, and look without condemnation upon the present."

Gene: What the Course means by letting the past go is to give the past a different interpretation than the one we are holding on to. How we do that is to give our past over to the Holy Spirit so it can be looked at in the light. In doing this, we see a different future by living in the present.

CHAPTER 115

Text, page 255: "The peace of God passeth your understanding."

A COURSE IN MIRACLES interpretation: "The peace of God passeth your understanding only in the past. Yet here it is, and you can understand it now."

Gene: When we listen to the Voice for God, we are in the present. In listening to the ego, we are always in the past and from that frame of reference we cannot hear the love that our Creator has for us.

CHAPTER 116

Text, page 257: "My peace I give you."

A COURSE IN MIRACLES interpretation: "In me you have already overcome every temptation that would hold you back. We walk together on the way to quietness that is the gift of God. Hold me dear, for what except your brothers can you need? We will restore to you the peace of mind, that we must find together. The Holy Spirit will teach you to awaken unto us and to yourself. This is the only real need to be fulfilled in time. Salvation from the world lies only here. My peace I give you. Take it of me in glad exchange for all the world has offered but to take away. And we will spread it like a veil of light across the world's sad face, in which we hide our brothers from the world, and it from them."

Gene: When we are one with Jesus, we are one with our Creator, and nothing the ego has to offer us will ever have any appeal to us. The reason for that is we will have no ego; and, therefore, cannot hear the voice opposite to God in every way. When we take the peace and love that Jesus offers us, we lift the veil that blocks our brothers and sisters from experiencing their peace.

CHAPTER 117

Text, page 302: "Hell"

A COURSE IN MIRACLES interpretation: "The Holy Spirit teaches thus: There is no hell. Hell is only what the ego has made of the present. The belief in hell is what prevents you from understanding the present, because you are afraid of it. The Holy Spirit leads as steadily to Heaven as the ego drives to hell."

Gene: There is no such thing as a literal place call hell. The feelings of hell exists only within the ego thought system. These thoughts only exists in the past, as that is the only place the ego lives. Its investment in the past assures a future like the past, thus avoiding the only place where we can experience peace and that's in the present.

CHAPTER 118

**Text, page 310: "Be humble before Him,
and yet great in Him."**

A COURSE IN MIRACLES interpretation: "And value
no plan of the ego before the plan of God. For you leave
empty your place in His plan, which you must fill if you
would join with me, by your decision to give to the world
for its release from littleness."

Gene: By listening to God, we fulfill our part in God's plan
for the release of any thought that would imprison his seem-
ingly separate sons and daughters. Our true strength lies in
accepting who we are as one with the Voice of God.

CHAPTER 119

Text, page 324: "Christmas"

A COURSE IN MIRACLES interpretation: "This is the season when you would celebrate my birth into the world. Yet you know not how to do it. Let the Holy Spirit teach you, and let me celebrate your birth through Him. The only gift I can accept of you is the gift I gave to you. Release me as I choose your own release. The time of Christ we celebrate together, for it has no meaning if we are apart.

The holy instant is truly the time of Christ. For in this liberating instant no guilt is laid upon the Son of God, and his unlimited power is thus restored to him. What other gift can you offer me, when only this I choose to offer you? And to see me is to see me in everyone, and offer everyone the gift you offer me. I am as incapable of receiving sacrifice as God is, and every sacrifice you ask of yourself you ask of me. Learn now that sacrifice of any kind is nothing but a limitation imposed on giving. And by this limitation you have limited acceptance of the gift I offer you.

It is in your power to make this season holy, for it is in your power to make the time of Christ be now. It is possible to do this all at once because there is but one shift in perception that is necessary, for you made but one mistake. It seems like many, but it is all the same.

The sign of Christmas is a star, a light in the darkness. See it not outside yourself, but shining in the Heaven within, and accept it as the sign the time of Christ has come. He comes demanding nothing. No sacrifice of any kind, of anyone, is asked of Him.

This Christmas give the Holy Spirit everything that would hurt you. Let yourself be healed completely that you may join with Him in healing, and let us celebrate our release together by releasing everyone with us.

Let no despair darken the joy of Christmas, for the time of Christ is meaningless apart from joy. Let us join in celebrating peace by demanding no sacrifice of anyone, for so you offer me the love I offer you. What can be more joyous than to perceive we are deprived of nothing? Such is the message of the time of Christ, which I give you that you may give it and return it to the Father, Who gave it to me. For in the time of Christ communication is restored, and He joins us in the celebration of His Son's creation."

Gene: Christmas is a time to join with Jesus in celebrating our Divine union with him. Let him join with us, through the process of forgiveness, to accomplish this most holy union. At this time, as well as all other times, we are to give Jesus the gift of our fear so he can remove it. This is the only gift Jesus wants from us. This giving entails no sacrifice. Through this removal process, we celebrate our birth as disciples of love. In celebrating this most joyous season, we re-establish our divine communication with Jesus as well as all our brothers and sisters.

Text, page 328: "The Prince of Peace"

A COURSE IN MIRACLES interpretation: "The Prince of Peace was born to reestablish the condition of love by teaching that communication remains unbroken even if the body is destroyed, provided that you see not the body as the necessary means of communication. And if you understand this lesson, you will realize that to sacrifice the body is to sacrifice nothing, and communication, which must be of the mind, cannot be sacrificed. The lesson I was born to teach, and still would teach to all my brothers, is that sacrifice is nowhere and love is everywhere. For communication embraces everything, and in the peace it reestablishes, love comes of itself."

Gene: One of the reasons Jesus allowed himself to go through the crucifixion was to show us, even when the body is laid aside, communication remains unbroken. He remains just as available to us now as he did when he walked this planet. Jesus did not sacrifice his body for us because sacrifice reinforces fear; but instead, showed us how to embrace love through life. As he tells us in Workbook lesson 70 "If it helps you, think of me holding your hand and leading you. And I assure you this will be no idle fantasy."

CHAPTER 121

Text, page 335: "By their fruits ye shall know them, and they shall know themselves."

A COURSE IN MIRACLES interpretation: "For it is certain that you judge yourself according to your teaching. The ego's teaching produces immediate results, because its decisions are immediately accepted as your choice. Cause and effect are very clear in the ego's thought system, because all your learning has been directed toward establishing the relationship between them. And would you not have faith in what you have so diligently taught yourself to believe? Yet remember how much care you have exerted in choosing its witnesses, and in avoiding those which spoke for the cause of truth and its effects."

Gene: Our perceptual world is determined exclusively by which voice we are listening to. Fruits are the projected thoughts we place on the world. Therefore, our world will bear the fruits of our thoughts.

CHAPTER 122

Text, page 350: "Lord's Prayer"

A COURSE IN MIRACLES interpretation: "Forgive us our illusions, Father, and help us to accept our true relationship with You, in which there are no illusions, and where none can ever enter. Our holiness is Yours. What can there be in us that needs forgiveness when Yours is perfect? The sleep of forgetfulness is only the unwillingness to remember Your forgiveness and Your Love. Let us not wander into temptation, for the temptation of the Son of God is not Your Will. And let us receive only what You have given, and accept but this into the minds which You created and which You Love. Amen"

Gene: In the Lord's prayer, Jesus is telling us to ask God to remove our fears and show us how to have a real relationship with our Creator, as well as our brothers and sisters. He is reminding us that we were created in His image and likeness, and that part of us needs no purification.

CHAPTER 123

Text, page 373: "Fear God"

A COURSE IN MIRACLES interpretation: "When you seem to see some twisted form of the original error rising to frighten you, say only, "God is not fear, but Love," and it will disappear. The truth will save you. It has not left you, to go out into the mad world and so depart from you. Inward is sanity; insanity is outside you. You but believe it is the other way; that truth is outside, and error and guilt within."

Gene: Our ego tells us never to look inside because of the tremendous fear that lies within. The reason the ego doesn't want us to look inside is because it knows that's where God dwells. No one would fear God if they associated God exclusively with love. In this interpretation of God, there is never a reason to fear God.

CHAPTER 124

Text, page 382: "Thy Will be done."

A COURSE IN MIRACLES interpretation: "Happy dreams come true, not because they are dreams, but only because they are happy. And so they must be loving. Their message is, "Thy Will be done," and not, "I want it otherwise."

Gene: Any thought we have has to manifest in our world. We have to start associating joy and peace with listening to the Voice for God. But any thought we have will produce something in our perceptual viewing screen.

Text, page 411: "Jesus died for our sins."

A COURSE IN MIRACLES interpretation: "I am made welcome in the state of grace, which means you have at last forgiven me. For I became the symbol of your sin, and so I had to die instead of you. To the ego sin means death, and so atonement is achieved through murder. Salvation is looked upon as a way by which the Son of God was killed instead of you. Yet would I offer you my body, you whom I love, knowing its littleness? Or would I teach that bodies cannot keep us apart? Mine was of no greater value than yours; no better means for communication of salvation, but not its Source. No one can die for anyone, and death does not atone for sin. But you can live to show it is not real."

Gene: To the ego, the guiltless are guilty. Since Jesus represented the greatest form of guiltlessness on the planet at that time, he had to die. An insane thought system produces insane results. No one can die for another's sins.

CHAPTER 126

Text, page 419: "Babe of Bethlehem"

A COURSE IN MIRACLES interpretation: "What danger can assail the wholly innocent? What can attack the guiltless? What fear can enter and disturb the peace of sinlessness? What has been given you, even in its infancy, is in full communication with God and you. In its tiny hands it holds, in perfect safety, every miracle you will perform, held out to you. The miracle of life is ageless, born in time but nourished in eternity. Behold this infant, to whom you gave a resting place by your forgiveness of your brother, and see in it the Will of God. Here is the babe of Bethlehem reborn. And everyone who gives him shelter will follow him, not to the cross, but to the resurrection and the life."

Gene: The babe of Bethlehem represents our innocence, and what can come to harm the totally innocent? We are to accept this infant as a mirror of ourselves. When we accept this into our lives, we become disciples for Jesus.

Text, page 425: "Easter"

A COURSE IN MIRACLES interpretation: "This is Palm Sunday, the celebration of victory and the acceptance of truth. Let us not spend this holy week brooding on the crucifixion of God's Son, but happily in the celebration of his release. For Easter is the sign of peace, not pain. A slain Christ has no meaning. But a risen Christ becomes the symbol of the Son of God's forgiveness on himself; the sign he looks upon himself as healed and whole.

This week begins with palms and ends with lilies, the white and holy sign the Son of God is innocent. Let no dark sign of crucifixion intervene between the journey and its purpose; between the acceptance of the truth and its expression. This week we celebrate life, not death. And we honor the perfect purity of the Son of God, and not his sins. Offer your brother the gift of lilies, not the crown of thorns; the gift of love and not the "gift" of fear. You stand beside your brother, thorns in one hand and lilies in the other, uncertain which to give. Join now with me and throw away the thorns, offering the lilies to replace them. This Easter I would have the gift of your forgiveness offered by you to me, and returned by me to you. We cannot be united in the crucifixion and in death. Nor can the resurrection be complete till your forgiveness rest on Christ, along with mine.

A week is short, and yet this holy week is the symbol of the whole journey the Son of God has undertaken. He started with the sign of victory, the promise of the resurrection, already given him. Let him not wander into the temptation of crucifixion, and delay him there. Help him to go in peace beyond it, with the light of his own innocence lighting his way to his redemption and release. Hold him not back with thorns and nails when his redemption is so near. But let the whiteness of your shining gift of lilies speed him on his way to resurrection.

Easter is not the celebration of the cost of sin, but of its end. If you see glimpses of the face of Christ behind the veil, looking between the snow-white petals of the lilies you have received and given as your gift, you will behold your brother's face and recognize it.

This Easter, look with different eyes upon your brother. You have forgiven me. This is the way to Heaven and to the peace of Easter, in which we join in glad awareness that the Son of God is risen from the past, and has awakened to the present."

Gene: Easter is the celebration of our release and celebration from the crucifixion/ego thoughts to our acceptance of the resurrection/Holy Spirit's thoughts. Easter is a sign of peace and forgiveness for Jesus, as well as all our brothers and sisters. Easter is the symbol of releasing our grievances towards others, as well as ourselves. When we offer forgiveness, we free ourselves as well as those whom we have forgiven.

Our willingness to unite with Jesus and remove our past hurts is a shining mirror for Easter to appear on this planet. Jesus is asking us to join with him so we can experience all that he sees in us.

CHAPTER 128

Text, page 517: "He is my own beloved son, in whom I am well pleased."

A COURSE IN MIRACLES interpretation: "For as His son's creation gave Him joy and witness to His Love and shared His purpose."

Gene: We all make up God's Son. God does not have just one offspring. There are a few places in the Course where they use the word Sonship; and technically, that is the word they should use all the time. We are one with God and one with Jesus. There is no difference between Jesus and all of us. God is well pleased with what She created. God created each and every one of us equally in Her eyes.

CHAPTER 129

Text, page 531: "Sin"

A COURSE IN MIRACLES interpretation: "Yet if the Holy Spirit can commute each sentence that you laid upon yourself into a blessing, then it cannot be a sin. Sin is the only thing in all the world that cannot change. It is immutable. And on its changelessness, the world depends. The magic of the world can seem to hide the pain of sin from sinners, and deceive with glitter and with guile. Yet each one knows the cost of sin is death. And so it is. For sin is a request for death, a wish to make this world's foundation sure as love, dependable as Heaven, and as strong as God Himself. The world is safe from love to everyone who thinks sin possible. Nor will it change. Yet is it possible what God created not should share the attributes of His creation, when it opposes it in every way?"

Gene: It is impossible to separate yourself from God, which is the definition of sin. But we can believe we have separated from God, our brothers and sisters, and everything else. This thought of sin is the cause of all our problems. What heals this thought of separation is a recognition of our true oneness with all our brothers and sisters. This joining is achieved through the process of forgiveness.

CHAPTER 130

Text, page 535: "Wrath of God."

A COURSE IN MIRACLES interpretation: "It is extremely hard for those who still believe sin meaningful to understand the Holy Spirit's justice. They must believe He shares their own confusion, and cannot avoid the vengeance that their own belief in justice must entail. And so they fear the Holy Spirit, and perceive the "wrath" of God in Him. Nor can they trust Him not to strike them dead with lightning bolts torn from the "fires" of Heaven by God's Own angry Hand."

Gene: There is no wrath of God because God is incapable of becoming angry. It was only men wanting to justify their own anger that caused them to project their unloving thoughts onto God. God is Love; and then you cease to speak. Remember the Course tells us we created God in our image. The more loving we become, the more loving experience of God we will allow in our lives.

CHAPTER 131

Text, page 661: "Your will be done."

A COURSE IN MIRACLES interpretation: "Only in arrogance could you conceive that you must make way to Heaven plain. The means are given you by which to see the world that will replace the one you made. Your will be done! In heaven as on earth this is forever true. It matters not where you believe you are, nor what you think the truth about yourself must really be. It makes no difference what you look upon, nor what you choose to feel or think or wish. For God Himself has said, "Your will be done." And it is done to you accordingly."

Gene: As Jesus said earlier, we are to become like little children. Little children recognize their total dependence on their Creator. Our will is always done, but which will are we listening to as we view the world? As the Course tells us, every thought produces something.

CHAPTER 132

Manual for Teachers, page 58: "Ask in the name of Jesus Christ."

A COURSE IN MIRACLES interpretation: "The Bible says, "Ask in the name of Jesus Christ." Is this merely an appeal to magic? A name does not heal, nor does an invocation call forth any special power. What does it mean to call on Jesus Christ? What does calling on his name confer? Why is the appeal to him part of healing?

We have repeatedly said that one who has perfectly accepted the Atonement for himself can heal the world. Indeed, he has already done so. Temptation may occur to others, but never to this One. He has become the risen Son of God. He has overcome death because he has accepted life. He has recognized himself as God created him, and in so doing he has recognized all living things as part of him. There is now no limit on his power, because it is the power of God. So has his name become the Name of God, for he no longer sees himself as separate from Him.

What does this mean to you? It means that in remembering Jesus you are remembering God. The whole relationship of the Son to the Father lies in him. His part in the Sonship is also yours, and his completed learning guarantees your own success. Is he still available for help? What did he say about this? Remember his promises, and ask yourself honestly whether it is likely that he will fail to keep them. The name of Jesus Christ as such is but a symbol. But it stands for love that is not of this world."

Gene: When we call upon Jesus we are actually calling upon God. The reason for this is that Jesus' thought system is completely connected to God's, and therefore, has no interference. He is available to all of us all the time. When we have removed our ego thought system, we will become just like Jesus. His purpose is to quicken this process.

CHAPTER 133

Manual for Teachers, page 68: "Resurrection"

A COURSE IN MIRACLES interpretation: "Very simply, the resurrection is the overcoming or surmounting of death. It is a reawakening or a rebirth; a change of mind about the meaning of the world. It is the acceptance of the Holy Spirit's interpretation of the world's purpose; the acceptance of the Atonement for oneself. The resurrection is the denial of death, being the assertion of life."

Gene: The resurrection is the overcoming of dead thoughts/ego thoughts. It is simply a change of thinking from our ego to the Voice for God. The Holy Spirit will reinterpret everything we see in the world for the purpose of peace, joy and happiness.

CHAPTER 134

Manual for Teachers, page 70: "Of myself I can do nothing."

A COURSE IN MIRACLES interpretation: "Here again is the paradox often referred to in the course. To say, "Of myself I can do nothing" is to gain all power. And yet it is but a seeming paradox. As God created you, you have all power. The image you made of yourself has none. The Holy Spirit knows the truth about you. The image you made does not."

Gene: "Of myself" would be referring to our false self, our ego, that thinks it knows all and is all. The part that is in constant communication with God, whether we are aware of it or not, is the part that allows us to accomplish everything our heart desires.

A PRAYER FOR PHYSICAL HEALING

I will use two fictitious names: Bob and Sue

Dear God of love,

Thank you for healing Sue's body to match her perfect Spirit. Lead her to the light and the peace of You in every cell, in every breath, in every beat of her heart. Open her mind to witness Your beauty, eternal perfection, now, tomorrow and always. Be with dear Bob and lift him to Your light past all fear, so that he can see Your work in Sue's and his life, and witness to the power of Your love, forever and ever.

Amen

To obtain additional copies write to:
Gene Skaggs, Jr.
1140 Riverwood Dr.
Nashville, Tn. 37216

Cell: (615) 969-6944
Website: www.onemiracle.org
Email: onemiracle@comcast.net

Retail: $15.00 (includes postage and handling)
ISBN: 978-0-9800049-0-8

Other books written by Gene Skaggs, Jr.

A BEGINNER'S GLOSSARY TO
A COURSE IN MIRACLES
Retail: $10.00 (includes postage and handling)

THE RELATIONSHIP GAME
CHANGING THE RULES
Retail: $12.00 (includes postage and handling)

101 QUESTIONS AND ANSWERS
ON THE COURSE
Retail: $14.00 (includes postage and handling)